500
Notable Cricket
Quotations

500

Notable Cricket

Quotations

COMPILED BY

Irving Rosenwater

'Cricket happens to be a game in which
deeds count a great deal,
and words very little.'
C. B. Fry, 1904

ANDRE DEUTSCH

First published in Great Britain by André Deutsch Limited
in a signed deluxe limited edition in 1995

This paperback edition first published in Great Britain in 1996

André Deutsch Limited
106 Great Russell Street
London WC1B 3LJ

ISBN 0 233 98981 1

CIP data available for this title from the British Library

Printed in Great Britain by
St Edmundsbury Press, Bury St Edmunds, Suffolk

CONTENTS

"The art of quotation requires more delicacy in the practice than those conceive who can see nothing more in a quotation than an extract."

Isaac D'Israeli

Preface

NOTHER book of quotations!
Yet why not? Did not H.S. Altham
once declare: 'Cricket is endless in
its appeal to those who love it and
understand it'? The broad sweep of
cricket history is fascinating from a myriad of view-
points, not least through the mouths of those who
have lived through its story contemporaneously. But
this is not one of those large, heavy books of quotations that are housed ponderously on reference
shelves. This book is small; and for that no apology is
made. It is designed to be read, and even enjoyed,
rather than to languish in academic reserve.

Quotations have been with us from the time when
man first spoke, and certainly from when he first
wrote. Cricket quotations are as old as the game
itself, even though most of them may be lost to us.
Ripe sayings of the Hambledonians were quoted by
John Nyren in 1832 (let us not forget that Nyren's
Hambledon reminiscences, in their *editio princeps* of
1833, were a reprint of articles that had already
appeared in a London journal, the *Town* newspaper,
in 1832).

The world of cricket writing is so vast that the task
of selection of entries for inclusion in this work has

been perhaps too easy — swamped by the *embarras de choix* that paradoxically throws a pall of despair over one's efforts.

One important feature has been adopted. Generally speaking no quotations have been taken from *books*, on the grounds that a great many cricket books are already on the shelves of cricket enthusiasts — and have (presumably) been read, thereby rendering any quotation from them already familiar. In any event books are *available*, and therefore their contents able to be referred to.

The best quotations should ideally be provocative, original and pithy. Unfortunately men do not go through their lives making utterances specially designed for quotations books — or perhaps fortunately, for a plethora of such utterances would soon become sadly dull and unworthy. At all events, for good or ill, we must make do with what there is: and there is indeed a great deal, so that any collection of quotations could very quickly multiply itself beyond reasonable proportions. To resist that, an arbitrary limit has been set — not the best solution, perhaps, but a practical one. For every quotation included, a dozen have fallen by the wayside — to be recovered maybe by a future compiler with his own views on inclusion and exclusion.

The quotations included here stretch back more than 150 years. Those that have survived the process of selection have done so principally through an original perspective or a critical acuity or a ration of wit or good humour or straightforward panache. In the nineteenth century many people seemed to speak, at least in print, with a ponderousness with which the times were associated. No doubt this was not actually so in common discourse: but the scribes managed to make it appear so. The nineteenth-century quotations thus have a lesser immediacy and sparkle than those of more recent times. For all that, the great majority of quotations here included are in some way arresting in their own right. They owe their presence to an appeal and an interest for a wide body of cricket lovers.

This book is a small personal collection of quotations which grew steadily over the years. Like any collection compiled by one person, it will betray the personal tastes of its begetter. However, if the reader finds some unexpected sayings, and derives some pleasure in the process, this little effort will have served its purpose.

IRVING ROSENWATER

LONDON, March 1995

SOURCES QUOTED

The Academy
The Advertiser (Adelaide)
The Age (Melbourne)
All England Cricket and Football
    Journal
The Antique Collector
Athletic News
Australasian Post
The Australian
Australian Playboy

The Badminton Magazine
Baily's Magazine
Bell's Life in London
Blackwood's Edinburgh
    Magazine
The Bulletin (Sydney)

Cab Trade News
The Captain
Cassell's Magazine
Chums
The Club Cricketer
Country Life
Cricket
The Cricketer
Cricketer (Melbourne)
The Cricketer Pakistan
The Cricketer (and Hockey) and
    Football Player
The Cricket Field

Daily Chronicle (Georgetown)
Daily Chronicle (London)
Daily Express
Daily Mail
Daily Mail Year Book
Daily Mirror
Daily News

Daily Sketch
Daily Star
Daily Telegraph (London)
Daily Telegraph (Sydney)
Daily Worker

The Empire Review
The Era
Evening News
Evening Post (Leeds)
Evening Standard
Everybody's

The Field
Financial Times
C.B. Fry's Magazine

The Globe
The Guardian (Manchester
    Guardian)
The Guardian (Sydney)
The Guiana Graphic
    (Georgetown)
Guiana Sportsman
    (Georgetown)

Hampstead & Highgate Express

The Independent
The Independent on Sunday
India Today

John O'London's Weekly

The Listener
Liverpool Daily Post
London Society
Longman's Magazine
Ludgate Monthly

The Mail on Sunday
Manchester Guardian
Men Only
The Morning Leader
Morning Post

National Review
New Review
The New Statesman and Nation
New York Times
New Zealand News
The News (Adelaide)
News Chronicle
News of the World
N.Z. Cricketer (Christchurch)

Observer
Occasion (Connaught Rooms
    Review)

Pall Mall Gazette
Pearson's Magazine
Picture Post
Playfair Cricket Monthly
Punch

Rand Daily Mail
    (Johannesburg)

St James's Budget
The Saturday Review
Sentry (St Vincent)
The Sketch
South Australian Register
    (Adelaide)
South Wales Daily News
The Sporting Globe
    (Melbourne)
Sporting Life
The Sporting Magazine

Sporting Record
Sports Events
The Sportsman
Sportsweek (Bombay)
Sportsweek's World of Cricket
    (Bombay)
The Star (Karachi)
The Star (London)
The Strand Magazine
The Sun (London)
The Sun (Melbourne)
The Sun (Sydney)
The Sun-Herald (Sydney)
Sunday Chronicle
Sunday Dispatch
Sunday Express
Sunday Mirror
Sunday Telegraph
Sunday Times (London)
Sunday Times (Perth, W.A.)
Sussex Daily News
The Sydney Mail
The Sydney Morning Herald

The Times
The Times Literary Supplement
The Times of India
Times Weekly (Bombay)
TNT Magazine (London)
Today
The Tribune (Chandigarh)

The Weekend Australian
The West Australian (Perth,
    W.A.)
Westminster Gazette
The Windsor Magazine
The World of Cricket
World Sports

Yorkshire Evening Post

"All I can suggest regarding the Test Match controversy is that Jardine should make Larwood bowl underhand."

A.W. Carr, January 1933

*

"I would have loved to have had a crack at them — when I was in my prime."

Harold Gimblett,
on Lillee and Massie, 1972

*

"The Australians should be grateful to Laker, though overwhelmed by him, for re-educating them in a science they have recently neglected."

Neville Cardus,
after J.C. Laker had taken
9−37 and 10−53 v Australia, Old Trafford, 1956

"An amateur as captain is advisable in every way, but such a captain should never hesitate to consult the judgment of his professional colleagues."

Lord Hawke, 1910

*

"I am sending him to England and I am confident that he will make a name."

K.S. Ranjitsinhji,
on his 14-year-old nephew,
K.S. Duleepsinhji

*

"After all, every good thing must come to an end. And the end ought to come when failures begin to affect you more than successes, as they have done in my case this season."

J.B. Hobbs,
during the final Test of his career, v Australia, Oval, 1930

*

"He uses his bat with almost the quickness of a Macartney or a Bradman."

William Pollock,
on Harold Gimblett (after his 67 not out v India, Lord's, 1936)

"I have urged his inclusion in the side, but never again will I do so. He went to one of the worst shots I have ever seen."

Harold Larwood,
on D.B. Close
(0 v Australia, Melbourne,
December 1950)

*

"Canterbury may have its trees and all the gay paraphernalia of the Festival, Maidstone its deer and rustic charm, Dover the beauty of its natural amphitheatre, and Cheltenham the classic dignity of the surrounding College. But who can wish for a more lovely sight than the Saffrons as you enter from the Town gate, the white pavilion, bordered with geraniums, framed in the background of the great hill, tall elms on one side, and Larkins Field, golden with buttercups, on the other."

E.W. Swanton, 1932

*

"We don't want to turn Lord's into a Coliseum. Every place of entertainment has its maximum capacity, and when that is reached the doors have to be closed."

Lord Harris, 1923

*

"It should have been done 10 years ago."

F.S. Trueman,
on Yorkshire's decision
[subsequently rescinded]
not to renew the contract of
G. Boycott, October 1983

*

"We never contemplated going our separate ways."

Eric Bedser,
on himself and his brother
Alec, 1990

*

"You came into the team as a lad in 1898, when you were only 20. It was a toss up then between you and another, but I am proud to think that our judgment proved correct."

Lord Hawke,
presenting Wilfred Rhodes
with his testimonial cheque,
April 1927

*

"There was no body-bowling in my day. We regarded cricket as a game, not a battle."

T.W. Garrett
(sole survivor of 1878
Australian touring team),
January 1933

"This thing can be done."

F.R. Spofforth,
to G. Giffen, with England
set 85 to win v Australia,
Oval, August 29, 1882

*

"Cricket is the litmus-paper of social and historical phases."

G.D. Martineau, 1935

*

"Ye gods! We coaches, I fear, are indeed a self-complacent lot. I often wonder how many of us can sleep o'nights!"

G.A. Faulkner, 1926

*

"Individuality is the soul of great cricket, and the coach, unless he is very careful, can smooth it out."

L.N. Constantine, 1943

*

"Compared with a catalogue of cricket items the headlines in the morning paper are uneventful."

L.E.S. Gutteridge, 1951

"Cricket has been too good a friend to me for nearly 70 years for me to part with it one moment before I have to."

Lord Harris,
on his 80th birthday, 1931

*

"I didn't see it, but I give him out!"

Umpire,
in reply to lbw appeal
against R.G. Barlow
(Royton v Littleborough),
April 25, 1891

*

"Oh for dear old Brentford!"

"Patsy" Hendren,
seasick, on board the
R.M.S. Osterley en route to
Australia, September 1920
(on being asked whether he
would prefer to be a foot-
baller rather than a sailor)

*

"A wicket-keeper's first care is for his hands. They are as valuable to him as are the legs of a ballet dancer."

R.T. Stanyforth, 1935

"I often wonder why the good old-fashioned fast yorker has been allowed to fade into the distance!"

G.A. Faulkner, 1923

*

"What's bred in the bone will come out in the shortest innings."

Neville Cardus, 1968

*

"Every summer you export on a temporary basis the incomparable Viv Richards who gives so much pleasure to cricket lovers all over Britain."

Queen Elizabeth II, addressing the people of Antigua, October 24, 1985, during a Royal tour of the eastern Caribbean

*

". . . English umpires may not be as good as they think they are . . ."

Robin Marlar, July 1992 (after the England v Pakistan Test at Old Trafford)

*

"If ever I was in any trouble I never had any hesitation in going to him. He always gave the professional player a square deal."

J.B. Hobbs,
on Lord Harris, on the day
of Lord Harris's death, 1932

*

"Men dole out runs as penuriously as misers dole out gold and dig themselves in as though they were laying the foundations of a cathedral. They are engaged not in a game, but in a business."

A.G. Gardiner, 1938

*

". . . I do not think the game has anything like the hold it had upon the public in my day."

T.W. Hayward
(aged 64), 1935

*

"I have known men cry off because they wanted to play in a lawn tennis tournament, or else wished to take a girl for a spin in a motor or in a punt on the river!"

H.D. Swan,
on "chucking" matches,
1925

*

"McDonald, the Australian fast bowler, now with Lancashire, advised me to send an order for bath-chairs to Perth, his idea being that after we had bowled for a little while under an Australian sun and on Australian wickets we should be semi-invalids."

A.E.R. Gilligan,
captain of M.C.C. side
to Australia, 1924–25,
September 13, 1924

*

"I trust that 'Connie' will not mind if I say that a lot of it was more like black magic than batting."

William Pollock,
on L.N. Constantine's 79 for
West Indies v England,
Oval, 1939

*

"If cricket's administrators are reluctant to grasp this particular nettle, a game which for more than a century has been the symbol of civilised behaviour could soon degenerate to the level of professional soccer and all-in wrestling."

Gerald Pawle,
on verbal intimidation on
the field, 1977

"Time was when we used to believe that sport and politics should be kept apart. The past 40 years have shown that to be idealistic nonsense . . ."

Robin Marlar, July 1992

*

"Complete freedom of speech may be a myth, but at least speech is freer in this country than anywhere else. You can curse royal garden parties when you are jammed by traffic in the Mall. You can even stick bills in your car window urging support for Rhodesia. And you will hear nothing about it from the Queen or the Prime Minister.

Free speech in cricket however is something you must forgo if you want to avoid hearing from MCC."

E.R. Dexter,
after being suspended for one month by MCC for publishing his autobiography without the prior consent of Sussex, 1966

*

"Denis Compton essays his slow left-hand from the Nursery, I nearly said the perambulator."

C.B. Fry,
aged 67, on D.C.S. Compton, aged 21, bowling for England v West Indies, Lord's, 1939

"There is a ridge at one end, and the batsmen were always looking for it, wondering whether they would be hit in the ear."

R.N. Harvey,
Australia's captain in
the Lord's Test, 1961, after
Australia's victory by five
wickets

*

"I could have saved all this torment and embarrassment if I had stayed home in the Cape. And so many other people would have been better off this winter."

Basil D'Oliveira,
on the cancelled 1968−69
MCC tour of South Africa,
September 1968

*

"This match will go down into history as one of the greatest Tests of all time. It is a pattern for everyone to follow."

R. Aird,
MCC secretary, in a tele-
gram to the captains in the
first tied Test (Australia v
West Indies, Brisbane),
December 14, 1960

"The more we watch cricket and the more we appreciate it, the more it bewilders us."

Sir Donald Bradman,
in London, May 1974

*

"But, my good man, even I cannot manufacture cricketers. We cannot pick players who are not there to pick."

P.A. Perrin,
qua England selector

*

"In my opinion the newspapers, over the years, have owed as much to first-class cricket for news-value as first-class cricket has owed to newspapers for publicity."

C.B. Fry, 1954

*

"Everyone likes to feel qua collector that they have something or other that no one else has, and it is for that reason that I suggest to my readers that if you collect curiosities of Cricket you will in nine cases out of ten, whether you spend much or little, succeed in getting something which happens to be the only one of its kind."

J.W. Goldman, 1937

"If only his commentaries were as accurate as his bowling."

Spectator at Grace Road, Leicester, on bowling of Jonathan Agnew (BBC cricket correspondent), re-called for NatWest Trophy semi-final v Essex, August 12, 1992

*

"The hurling of the ball at a batsman's head four times an over is certainly not cricket."

Viscount Cobham (former captain of Worces-tershire), Governor-General of New Zealand, at London New Zealand Cricket Club dinner, the Drapers' Hall, London, May 18, 1960

*

"A bowler should think and look where he means to drop each ball he bowls. Half the wild bowling that one sees in junior games comes from sheer inatten-tion, like putting an active for a passive in Latin prose."

H.S. Altham, 1949

*

"What a pity we cannot publish fielding averages!"

Olympian,
in *The Sketch*, August 22,
1894

*

"It is surprising to learn that one of the richest cricket counties — Yorkshire — has lost 2,500 members since 1930. In that year there were 8,000 members; now there are about 5,500. What will the committee do about it?"

The Clubman,
in *Daily Mirror* (London),
July 4, 1932

*

"We play Test cricket not only to match our skill, but also as great fun."

M.A. Chidambaram,
President, Indian Cricket
Board of Control, 1962

*

"Seldom in connection with any cricket project has condemnation been so general and so outspoken."

Sydney Pardon,
on the proposed scheme of
Lord Hawke to divide the
counties into two divisions,
1910

"It's time someone stood up to be counted and acted as a spokesman for the players."

Allan Lamb,
on alleged ball-tampering,
August 1992

*

". . . in the nets alongside the silvery Severn, the Yorkshire bowlers queue up to satisfy once more this original, stubborn, self-absorbed, and truly astonishing old soldier's appetite for batting."

Frank Keating,
on Geoffrey Boycott at
Worcester, at the start of
Boycott's 21st full season of
championship cricket, 1983

*

"Umpires and scorers at Lord's shall be paid as usual – the former £2 each, and the latter £1 each. But in the event of a match at Lord's lasting but one day, the umpires and scorers to be paid only half those sums."

M.C.C. committee
resolution, 1846

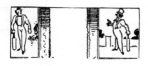

*

"We know as much of the history of cricket as we shall ever know now, and we have been told everything relating to the science of the game. There is no fresh ground to be explored."

Rev. R.S. Holmes, 1893

*

"You can't expect people to play as well at Test level as they would if they didn't have to play several one-day matches. In order to keep up the quality of the Test matches we shouldn't have so many one-day internationals."

J.M. Brearley,
in Melbourne, February 1980 (at the close of the England tour of Australia, 1979–80)

*

"Well, perhaps, my dear fellow, you ought to leave the window open . . ."

Legendary response
of C.I. Thornton to complaining owner, through whose window two successive balls have been hit

*

"Give up cricket. Go and play tennis with Betty Nuthall."

K.S. Ranjitsinhji,
in a telegram to his nephew
K.S. Duleepsinhji (during a
lean spell)

*

"Never treat bowling lightly, and, no matter how bad it may be, always play the strict game, and play every ball in the same way as if it had been delivered by the best bowler of the day."

W.L. Murdoch, 1882

*

"You know the cricketing enthusiasm of this part of the world. We don't play in November, but there is scarcely any other time of the year when bat and ball is not somewhere to be found."

J.M. Kilburn,
writing from Yorkshire,
1943

*

"If, as many people contend, club captains are apt to delay their declarations unnecessarily, there is great fun in getting runs against the clock . . ."

A.W.T. Langford,
on club cricket, 1932

"Faster than Ernie Jones? Why, if you put Gregory on the top of McDonald, they would not be as fast as Ernie, and I know."

> Hanson Carter,
> on the suggestion that Gregory and McDonald were "much faster" than Jones, 1921

*

"BOWLERS WANTED. – Fast, Fast-medium, medium or slow, leg-break, left or right handed. Should be between 25 and 30 years of age, strong physique essential. Only the very highest class suitable for the posts offered."

> Proposed advertisement of I.A.R. Peebles, for England's selectors, 1949

*

"I don't like the look of that bat, George; it seems as if he means mischief this time."

> Wilfred Rhodes,
> to George Hirst, on V.F.S. Crawford coming out with a very dark and apparently heavy bat for Surrey v Yorkshire, Bradford, 1901, after a first-innings duck. Crawford scored 110 out of 174

"It is impossible to judge from performances in county cricket whether any player — save the obviously great, such as Hammond — will be any good in a Test match. County cricket nowadays does not challenge either character or a comprehensive technique."

Neville Cardus, 1938

*

". . . when matches are once contracted for, they should not be cancelled except under the most pressing circumstances."

Club Cricket Conference Executive Council resolution, December 2, 1932

*

"I wonder what the Eskimos are doing next summer."

W.J.O'Reilly, contemplating Australia's cricket "skill", January 1986

"I was never considered good enough for the school eleven, so up to the age of fifteen, when I joined the Sussex Nursery, I had had very little match experience."

M.W. Tate, 1927

*

". . . he has shown how, all other issues set aside, a team is never done with till its hitter is out, and also that no side should be without a hitter. Future selection committees, please note!"

W.J. Ford,
on G.L. Jessop, after his 104
for England v Australia,
Oval, 1902

*

"It is fast becoming — nay, I believe I do not exaggerate when I say it has become — one of the greatest mediums for gambling in the kingdom."

George Lacy,
1897, on the County Championship

*

"I heard of more than one case in which as much as thirty shillings was charged for bed, breakfast, and dinner during the Test at Nottingham."

F.S. Ashley-Cooper,
1930 (on cricketers' fees
and expenses)

"Someone the other day said I must feel tremendous pressure from the press. I don't because I don't read it."

E.R. Dexter,
1989, as chairman of Test selectors

*

"Truly is this master spinner the wonder of his age, and yet not good enough for Test cricket!"

"Old Ebor" (A.W. Pullin), on A.P. Freeman, 1932, after Freeman had taken 5-88 and 8-56 v Lancashire and 8-31 and 9-61 v Warwickshire in four days' cricket for Kent

*

"Ten Little Aussie Boys Lakered in a Row"

Headline
after J.C. Laker's 10-53 v Australia, Old Trafford (*Daily Express*, August 1, 1956)

"Just think. All those physios I'm putting out of work."

G.R. Dilley,
on the day he announced
his retirement, 1992

*

"There has not been a single good wicket at Lord's as yet this season . . . It is almost an insult to common sense to suppose that a Club with an income of ten thousand a year cannot find the means of covering half-a-dozen acres with turf adapted to the game of cricket."

The *Saturday Review*, 1873, reporting the University match

*

"Why is there no Test match played in the West of England?"

C. Dixon,
of Exeter, in a letter to the
Athletic News, 1930

*

"In my very early days bowling appealed to me more than any other branch of cricket."

Herbert Strudwick, 1911

"They are certainly a mysterious side — and I cannot help thinking they may one day do something surprising."

E.H.D. Sewell,
on the West Indian touring side, 1906

*

"A cricket Blue, by the way, was telling me the other day of his experience on the beach at Dunkirk. He said that one of the things that impressed him was that it would have been possible to pick up two first-class 'Gentlemen v. Players' sides."

Daily Telegraph, 1940

*

"It's a hell of a shock."

Mark Haslam,
19-year-old Auckland spinner, with 11 first-class wickets at 38, on being selected for New Zealand's tour of Zimbabwe and Sri Lanka, September 1992

*

"There can be no doubt that umpires' decisions have this year given rise to a deal of dissatisfaction; but was it *ever* different?"

Rev. R.S. Holmes, 1894

"One is tempted to dream that in Utopia it will be a criminal offence to play games after one is twenty-five."

Geoffrey Weald, 1932

*

"I often wonder how much Hobbs and Sutcliffe might have needed to change their defensive methods if confronted by contemporary off-spinners and the law that is now so strongly the ally of this kind of bowling."

Neville Cardus, 1952

"One of the great difficulties with which everybody who superintends a big ground has to contend is not caused by the state of the wicket so much as the state of mind of some of the batsmen, who, as everybody knows, are often bowled out before they go to the wickets in important matches."

Percy Pearce,
Ground   Superintendent,
Lord's, 1897

*

"Mr — was a member of the M.C.C. and often went to Lord's. Mr Gilbert Beyfus, Q.C. for Mrs — : Did he discuss cricket intelligently? — To tell the truth I used to get him a cushion and, like all the other old gentlemen there, he went to sleep."

Report in *News Chronicle*

*

". . . not only in Test match cricket, but in first-class cricket generally, it is the veterans who count most."

A.H.J. Cochrane, 1930

*

"The cricket ground was enclosed at each end with booths, and all up the Forest hill were scattered booths and tents, with flags flying, fires burning, pots boiling, ale-barrels standing, and asses, carts, and people bringing still more good things. There were plenty of apple and ginger-beer stalls; and lads going round with nuts and with waggish looks crying, 'Nuts, lads! Nuts, lads!' "

William Howitt, on the Nottinghamshire v Sussex match on the Forest ground, Nottingham, 1835

*

"The fact is that cricket has become less of a sport and more of a business. A cricket match is no longer a game, but a strife."

George Lacy,
1897, on past and present

*

"It is a book as lasting as the hills and as permanent a landmark. It is as immortal as W.G. himself."

L.E.S. Gutteridge,
1951, on Nyren's *Young Cricketer's Tutor* and *The Cricketers of my Time*

*

"As an American I had supposed that baseball was the more strenuous and demanding game, cricket by comparison a pastime of softies. Not so, I discovered. Baseball, on the contrary, is simplistic, draughts as compared with chess."

John Paul Getty II, 1992

*

"Find out where the ball is. Go there. Hit it."

K.S. Ranjitsinhji's
three imperatives on batsmanship

"It sounds strange to me to hear, as I often do, that our fast bowlers nowadays are only good for four or five overs and then must be nursed. What would Sammy Woods say?"

E.J. Metcalfe, 1932

*

"Do you honestly think that Geoffrey Boycott would rather play golf than play in a Test match? Anyone who knows me the tiniest bit and who thinks that must be totally crackers!"

Geoffrey Boycott
to Frank Keating, 1983, on
Boycott's playing golf on
one of the days of his final
Test (Calcutta, January
1982)

*

"Suggestion that Lord's Cricket Ground be used as a greyhound racing track in winter is almost sacrilegious. As well suggest Westminster Abbey as a cinema when a service is not being held."

Letter in *Sunday Express*

"I love writing on, and reading about cricket. I go into my study after breakfast and except for an interval for lunch of about an hour I work all day. It is a great delight to me."

F.S. Ashley-Cooper

*

"We hadn't realised the gulf between a minor county and the first-class game."

Don Robson, chairman, Durham C.C.C., after the county finished bottom of the County Championship in its first season, 1992

*

"How marvellous, how English, how incredible they are, sitting in patient ignorance of all that is going on, and yet strangely and inwardly contented, realising deep down in their unconsciousness that they are taking a vague but real part in some ritual of beauty."

Dudley Carew, on spectators at county matches, 1928

*

*

"Like the Church of England, cricket is very much –
perhaps too much – in the hands of a bureaucracy. It
is not the Dean of St Paul's or Don Bradman who
makes the headlines today, but decisions taken at
Church House about women preachers, or at Lord's
about South Africa."

W.F. (Lord) Deedes, 1990

*

"By judiciously mixing back and forward play a
batsman can bring his 'blind spot' to the verge of
complete elimination, and thus remove a fruitful
cause of balls batsmen do not like."

J.B. Hobbs, 1913

*

"They were with us from the beginning of the war;
we were nearly run out in the first over, and all the
spectators said we were out, but Umpire Churchill
said 'No'."

Lt.-Col. R.T. Stanyforth in
speech of welcome to 1948
Australian side, British
Sportsman's Club lun-
cheon, Savoy Hotel, Lon-
don, April 1948

"The most important thing he taught me was to always tell the truth in life. He said if I made any mistakes I could expect to get punished for them. Then I would have to get on with it and make sure I didn't make the same mistakes again."

I.M. Chappell on his father,
A.M. Chappell, on his
death, April 1984

*

"I don't care if he was standing on his head."

D.G. Bradman's
reply to a critic who re-
marked that his (Bradman's)
son's feet were wrongly
positioned when he hit a
ball to the boundary

*

"It is impossible to predicate of any given match that it is the most sensational, or of any cricket victory that it is the most remarkable on record; but few matches or victories can have deserved superlatives more, the strange thing being not that we won, but that the Australians lost, so keenly clever are they to press an advantage. The truth is, that we never looked like winning till Rhodes's last stroke."

W.J. Ford,
on England's one-wicket
victory over Australia at the
Oval, 1902

"The adults, men and women, need and want heroes, idols. They want to believe that I am doing all the things that they cannot do — the whole wine, women and song routine."

Imran Khan,
in Lahore, 1983

*

"The Englishman's interest in cricket springs, I believe, from a devotion to the game's simplicity bred in the English countryside — and, even at the highest level, he wishes this basic virtue to be apparent."

S.C. Griffith,
secretary, MCC, 1963

*

"There was more fair play in the old Prize Ring of the past than there is in some of the cricket of the present."

Fred Gale, 1897

*

"The batsman nowadays is 'top dog'. Top dressings and artificial preparations have reduced the bowler to helplessness."

Charles Shaw Baker, 1910

"We expect there will be acute analysis of batting, bowling, fielding and captaincy, but we do not think the game should be used as a vehicle for distortion or exaggeration of events."

D.G. Bradman,
at Cricket Writers' Club
dinner, April 1948

*

". . . as a cricket raconteur he is supreme, and the stern rigidity of print can never hope to reproduce the rich humour, the unsparing but withal kindly wit, the volcanic laughter of Sam!"

R.C. Robertson-Glasgow,
on S.M.J. Woods, following
the publication of *My
Reminiscences*, 1925

*

"Strudwick, disguised as a huge ape, caused immense amusement attached to Simpson-Hayward's organ (the latter was a Piedmontese organ-grinder), and certainly the Surrey wicket-keeper played his part in very realistic fashion, while Bird as a 'Coon' and Tufnell as a Persian nobleman had capital dresses."

Captain E.G. Wynyard,
on fancy dress ball aboard
R.M.S. *Saxon*, en route to
South Africa, with MCC
team, 1909

*

"There have got to be changes."

M.P. Murray,
chairman, Structure Work-
ing Party on first-class game,
1992

*

"Personally, I am rather inclined to think that the average county side to-day is not as good as those I played against on any of my previous tours of England. With the sole exception of Yorkshire, who were deprived of what looked like victory through rain at Bramall Lane, the counties generally have presented us with little or no opposition."

W.A. Oldfield
(who toured England as a
player in 1919, 1921, 1926,
1930 and 1934) in radio
broadcast, August 1938

*

"I doubt if there have ever been more independent and fearless umpires in county cricket than we have at present; umpires do not hesitate about giving a man out if their mind is made up."

Lord Hawke, 1910

*

"On all wickets, in England, Australia, and South Africa, on turf and on matting, fine weather or foul, Jack Hobbs for a quarter of a century went his way, always the supreme batsman, in spite of all changes of technique and tactics. He was the great arch or bridge over which cricket of the Golden Age of Grace strode into the twentieth century."

Neville Cardus,
in radio broadcast to mark
70th birthday of J.B. Hobbs,
December 1952

*

"Why, there is as big a gap between even the best club cricket and county cricket as there is between county cricket and Test-match cricket."

Sir Home Gordon, 1928

*

"To my mind there are very few fast bowlers now, though there are plenty of fine fast throwers."

Dr. E.M. Grace, 1894

"It is only their love of the noble game that keeps cricket book collectors from growing old before their time."

L.E.S. Gutteridge, 1951

*

"Playing Shield cricket in Australia was much closer to playing in Tests, whereas I didn't find playing a three-day game against a weak county just before a Test very good preparation."

G.A. Hick,
looking back on his first series of Test cricket, when he averaged 10.71 in four Tests v West Indies, 1991

*

"Use every device, and all your cunning, to make your lads appreciate the full value of a straight bat, O Parents!"

G.A. Faulkner, 1925

*

"I don't attempt to deny that I am and always was a lazy bowler; until a crisis comes I don't seem to be able to do my very best."

F.R. Spofforth, 1892

"He was such a hero, alike with elderly businessmen in the pavilion and shrilly screeching schoolboys scampering excitedly all round the ground, that the other players became like chorus nonentities acting as a backcloth to a great star."

Frank Rostron,
on J.C. Laker's 10 wickets in
an innings and 19 wickets in
the match v Australia, Old
Trafford, 1956

*

"Cricket in general, and bowling in particular, has seldom been at such a low ebb in this country, and it behoves all those in any authoritative position to try and put their counties in order."

G.J.V. Weigall, 1935

*

"From John Nyren down to Mr Cardus writing on cricket has been better than on any other pastime."

Bernard Darwin, 1941

*

"Mr Chairman and Gentlemen – I am a doer, and not a talker."

J.J. Lyons
(the words comprising an
entire after-dinner speech)

"I still feel convinced that a superannuation scheme, such as I suggested to the committee of the M.C.C. two years ago, would be better than the present system of benefit matches; which is particularly hard on some umpires who, when they are put off the list, have nothing to fall back upon, and are left to starve in their old age."

Alfred Shaw, 1900

*

"It is time for Kim Hughes to stop talking about using a psychologist in the dressing room. It is time to stop talking about the 'new professionalism'. It is time to stop talking about not hooking. It is time for Kim Hughes to stop talking."

I.M. Chappell,
after Australia's defeat by West Indies by an innings and 112 runs at Perth, November 1984

*

"There, it shows what you umpires are all worth!"

E. Peate
(Yorkshire), after he had deliberately thrown a ball v Lancashire, Old Trafford, and not been no-balled, 1883

"I'm sorry, ladies and gentlemen, I'm not a plumber."

H.D. Bird (umpire),
countering spectators' criticism on play being halted
after two overs when bowler's run-up was found to be
flooded, England v West Indies, Headingley, 1988

*

"With the conditions as they are — grassy pitches, lush outfields, and expert ball shining processes — some legal and some not so legal — who can blame them?"

S.C. Griffith,
secretary, MCC, on county cricketers playing in the way
most likely to pave the way for victory, 1963

*

"Perhaps if our wickets had been as good as the wickets are now, there wouldn't be much to choose between them."

Tom Adams,
comparing Fuller Pilch and W.G. Grace, 1893

*

". . . I like bowling immensely. When I was captain at Cambridge I bowled so much at one end that it became known as Wilson's end."

E.R. Wilson, 1905

*

"Of course, I haven't! According to what some of them say, it would take me about a fortnight to do it!"

Joe Vine,
on being reminded he had never reached 200 for Sussex, 1913. (He did so in 1920, aged 45)

*

"Barring the most catastrophic occurrence, the sort of thing that has never happened before at the Casino, I am bound to win. My system is 99 per cent certain."

Roy Webber,
cricket statistician, on his "system" to win at roulette at Monte Carlo, 1958. (The "system" failed)

"Never has a subject been so pushed, pulled, knocked down, set up again, bounced and consequently exhausted as, to plagiarise our friends the Press, has been our dear old national pastime."

R.C. Robertson-Glasgow, on the year's output of cricket literature, 1925

*

"The Captain reported that rabbits were burrowing under the pavilion, and various ways of getting rid of them were discussed."

Lessness Park C.C. minute book, 1910

*

"Commercialism and other factors have taken over and I think that if you want to see gentlemanly cricket you have to go back to the village green."

B.A. Johnston, 1992

*

" 'Moaners', cried most Australians when the British press complained that Australian Ian Meckiff threw the ball. Now our own moaners are on the job."

Daily Telegraph (Sydney) editorial, on assertions by Richie Benaud and Robert Gray in Kingston that C.C. Griffith was a "thrower", 1965

"The narrow bat will do little, if anything, to cure the evils of professionalism; but it will, undoubtedly, have the effect of making innings and scores shorter, and so bringing matches to a quicker close."

Horace G. Hutchinson,
in support of a proposal for
a narrower bat, 1900

*

"Really, we shouldn't be playing cricket on this wicket for another 12 months."

A.R. Border,
captain of Australia, two
days before the Perth Test v
New Zealand, November
1985. (Australia lost by six
wickets)

*

"I believe the return of three-day games — the Tests are a law unto themselves — is not only improbable but unthinkable. Nobody is likely to have all that time at his disposal . . ."

H.T. Cozens-Hardy,
in a letter to *The Cricketer*,
1943

*

"Nationalism in cricket is growing fast as Commonwealth ties loosen, and a watch will have to be kept on behaviour on the field under the pressures that huge crowds, especially in hot countries, generate. It may well prove necessary to examine and revise the method of appointing Test match umpires and particularly to seek to ensure that standards are raised, and raised to the level of those of the best."

C.G. Howard, 1973

*

"We all grow old, but a great delight of cricket is that as long as you live and can see, the joys of looking on at the game never decline."

Hon. R.H. Lyttelton, 1898

*

"I am not making excuses, but every English captain for years back has been a flop from the cricket point of view. I want to thank you for your wonderful kindness, even though you may have ruined me as a cricketer."

G.O. Allen,
in speech of thanks following presentation of set of studs and cuff links, fifth Test v Australia, Melbourne, third day, March 1, 1937

*

"This is ample revenge for the year of our national disgrace, 1878, when the second Australian team got the M.C.C. out for 19. Everything comes to those who wait."

"Rover",
in *The Morning Leader*, after the M.C.C. had dismissed the Australians at Lord's for 18, 1896

"Australian groundsmen should be out with their scissors and their mowers, snipping away to help Bob Holland and Greg Matthews. Later, if they're embarrassed, they can blame the cane toads."

Peter Roebuck,
encouraging groundsmen in Australia to take advantage of home fixtures, 1985

*

"For myself I can say that there is too much talking and writing about the decline of cricket."

J.T. Tyldesley, 1911

"Ten years ago there was never the slightest suspicion of this barracking evil at Lord's."

P.F. Warner,
on the prevalence of iron-
ical barracking by crowds at
Lord's, 1908

*

"All I can do now, unfortunately, is to remember the way it used to be — and to enjoy the continuing friendship of teammates like Len Darling, Leo 'Mo' O'Brien, Bill Ponsford, Keith Rigg, Bill Brown and, of course, Lindsay Hassett. There is a tremendous bond between us old geezers that only death can end."

W.J. O'Reilly,
six days after his 80th birthday, 1985

*

"I wish we could choose it, but as all the players have to pay their own expenses between this country and Australia it's not so much a question of choosing as asking anyone who has the time and the money to submit her name, and then, from those volunteers, building up the best team possible."

Marjorie Pollard,
in   radio   broadcast   on
women's cricket and prop-
osed   1939–40   W.C.A.
team to Australia, August
1938

"Good fielding makes weak bowling strong."

Lord Hawke

*

"My father was no great lover of the cricket establishment."

Tim Arlott,
on the failure of his father,
John Arlott, to bequeath any
of his cricket collection to
MCC, 1992

*

"My old action was like Jeff Thomson's, except he knew where the ball was going and I did not."

Imran Khan,
on his 1973 change of
action, 1980

*

"Cricket records, like Aunt Sallies, exist primarily to be knocked down. In part this accounts for the optimism with which most cricketers are endowed when facing long odds."

D.R. Jardine, 1937

*

"That the batting is not so attractive I think there can be no two opinions. Hits nowadays are almost confined to drives, snicks, cuts, and occasional pulls."

George Lacy,
on past and present, 1897

*

"Fondest memories of Hampshire cricket at Bournemouth."

Card beside a red rose placed on the pitch at Dean Park at the close of the ground's final first-class match, August 20, 1992

*

"Someone talking out of the fulness of his ignorance, I should imagine!"

H.D. Swan,
chairman, Essex, on the suggestion that Essex should play elsewhere in the county besides Leyton, 1913

*

"So far as I am concerned, it has not made my task as an umpire any more difficult; in fact, easier."

Bill Reeves,
on introduction of lbw (N.), 1935

*

"When the public are drawn together by the attraction of sounding names, and witness no better play than that of Tuesday last, at the Oval, they consider that their time is wasted, and so do we."

The Era,
on the performance of the Honourable Artillery Company (42 and 65) in its match v the South London Club (177), 1848

*

"If I were asked for the typical champagne batsmen, I should divide my vote between Mr Spooner and Mr Trumper."

Sir Home Gordon, 1908

*

"Arguably the saddest feature of the new season has been the revelation by Barry Richards that he evidently finds building an innings these days about as satisfying as working on a factory assembly-line."

Will Price,
Evening Post (Leeds), 1978

*

"Convinced that your wise and humane presence would be invaluable in the House of Commons."

Cable (portion)
from Jeremy Thorpe, Liberal leader, to Sir Learie Constantine, asking if he would stand as Liberal candidate in by-election at Nelson and Colne, 1968

*

"Cheat is a very ugly word, but the whole question is, to me, like negotiating some of the juicier passages of the Old Testament, and then asking if Jehovah was a just man."

Ian Peebles,
on the question "Was Dr. W.G. Grace a cheat?",
1951

*

"I wonder whether the great Ranji would have found his favourite glance a business proposition with as many deft hands round the corner as one sees today."

E.W. Swanton,
on the preponderance of leg slip fielders, 1971

"The trouble with the game in this country is that everyone is far too conservative."

Clive Rice,
criticised in South Africa for posing for an advertisement clad only with a St. Christopher medallion around his neck and a bat held strategically in front of him, 1980

*

"I conceive, after careful consideration, that there is only one course open for me to adopt, and that is, to advise the Committee of Kent County Cricket Club to decline any further engagement with your club, certainly for this year, and until a more satisfactory state of things maintains."

Lord Harris,
in letter to Lancashire C.C.C., on their continuing to play Crossland and Nash, bowlers with doubtful actions, 1885

*

"To meet you in frock coat and silk hat one would never think that you score many runs. How deceptive are appearances."

Albert Craig
("Surrey Poet"), in open letter to P.F. Warner, 1907

"We have seen many men in that position who have been so imbued with the ideas of good fellowship, and so chained by the duty to avoid 'trouble', that they have at times laid themselves open, by their complaisance, to the charge of imperilling the good work done by their men on the field."

P.G.H. Fender,
on choosing an
England captain for a tour to
Australia, 1934

*

"I just told the players there was a phone call and everybody was in stitches."

H.D. Bird,
umpire in one-day International at Old Trafford, when
halting play on the ringing
of a mobile telephone handed to him earlier by I.T.
Botham, 1992

*

"His hands were the biggest ever seen on a cricket field and possibly in any other sphere. It was said that he could pick up a wet soccer ball one-handed, a tale which I personally can well believe, having seen a cricket ball disappear entirely in those awe-inspiring fingers."

I.A.R. Peebles,
on A.W. ("Dave") Nourse,
1947

"I suppose if we lose I shall be the next scapegoat."

D.B. Close,
after being appointed England's third captain of the
1966 series v West Indies,
with England 3-0 down,
Oval, 1966. (England won
by an innings and 34 runs)

*

"I have never believed that any player should be
nursed from responsibilities, for the only way to
improve is under stress."

P.M. Pollock, 1970

*

"I think that more men stand and hit fast-footed now;
but I don't think that so many of them play a perfect
game. There is hardly one out of ten of the best
batsmen who uses the whole of his bat."

Alfred Shaw, 1900

*

"How I hate those averages! I have done so all my
life."

Lord Hawke, 1914

*

"I have ridden so many kilometres in the past year I reckon I could have entered for the Melbourne to Warrnambool bike race."

Ian Redpath,
on his training schedule to return to cricket, after a serious injury, October 1978

*

"However, if it be true — and it *is* true — that England possesses the two greatest batsmen in the world, Hutton and Compton, it is just as true that Australia can point to the most dangerous of all living bowlers, Lindwall."

Neville Cardus, November 1954

*

"Cricket is still only a game and I am sure that many spectators share my distaste for the extravagant displays by some members of fielding sides as and when wickets are taken. Bowlers are employed to take wickets and fielders are expected to take catches, so when either one is successful histrionics are unnecessary . . ."

Jim Clarke,
Hon. Secretary, Lancashire Cricket League, in his annual report on 1986 season, 1987

*

"I shall be very willing to start a subscription with a modest sum of five shillings. This neglect of past worthies pains me."

Rev. R.S. Holmes,
on the deteriorating monu-
ment to William Lillywhite
in Highgate Cemetery, 1892

*

"I suppose I was born to give it a go."

Harold Gimblett, 1972

*

"The game between King Cross and Brighouse, at Halifax, was interrupted because Mr Grahame-White, in his flight across the town, where he is giving exhibitions of aviation this week-end, passed directly over the ground, and he received great cheers from the players and spectators."

Athletic News, 1910

*

"Cricket officials in Sydney are at their wits' end trying to find enough grounds for teams to use and enough teams for players to join."

Richie Benaud, 1972

"Admitting, for the sake of argument, that the umpires — or some of them — are afraid to no-ball men, my remedy for this is that these umpires should be dropped, and others found who would do their duty."

P.F. Warner,
on the "throwing question",
1901

*

"It's all over for me now, Kipps, it's all over."

C.L. Walcott,
at the end of his final day as
a first-class cricketer, to
umpire Cecil P. Kippins,
Georgetown, 1964

*

"It does not necessarily follow that inclusion in a county match makes a player a first-class cricketer in reality. Hardly that."

G.L. Jessop, 1911

*

"It seems to be a fact to-day that cricket is the only high-class game of skill and pace in which its participants take no pains whatever to train except in the actual playing of it."

G.J.V. Weigall,
on players' fitness, 1935

"I am sure we have got to consider the spin bowler and his needs in such a way as to ensure that he is at least as important to a side as the seam bowler."

S.C. Griffith,
secretary, MCC, 1963

*

"What you must realise is that players are not machines. They are humans like everybody else, and as such, make mistakes."

J.V. Coney,
captain, 1985–86 New Zealand team in Australia, November 1985

*

"*In primis*, let us start with this indisputable position — that there arrives a time in life when cricket becomes a toil and a humiliation, while golf, until the very grave, remains a glory and a joy."

Horace G. Hutchinson,
on "Cricket v Golf", 1890

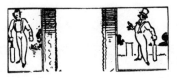

*

"Cricket, which, though it's supposed to have bound Empires together, has caused — and, with luck, will continue to cause — more arguments, public and private, than politics and women."

R.C. Robertson-Glasgow,
1949

*

". . . even when he is being stubborn Milton retains his elegance — a batsman of trimmed Cotswold stone."

Alan Gibson,
on C.A. Milton (Gloucester-
shire), 1970

*

"The fielding of the English team I saw in the final Test at the Oval last year was disgraceful. I wonder what the old Oval crowd would have said if the Surrey team of my day had gone about their fielding in that way."

T.W. Hayward,
1935 (on England v Austra-
lia Test, Oval, 1934)

*

"There are moments when the large crowd dwells in such suspense over the contest between bat and ball that the community of interest seems to create electric waves of sympathy between the individual spectators."

Sir Home Gordon, 1908

*

"You did not really reckon his innings in runs; it was so many minutes, or hours, of beauty."

"Old Fag",
on F.E. Woolley, in *John O' London's Weekly*, 1938

*

"Cricket can only avoid losing its best talent after the war by co-operating with the leagues instead of still regarding them as poor relations."

L.V. Manning,
January 1945

*

". . . the sun is streaming from a Pacific blue sky, and I have just been watching cricket in the Parks at Oxford on a May morning; and the Parks at Oxford on such a day of warmth and blossom is a foretaste of heaven."

Neville Cardus, 1953

"Once again we have the pleasure of welcoming to South Australia a group of bright young Englishmen eager to learn something of the game of cricket. Well, they have come to the right place. If there is one spot on the verdant globe where cricket can be taught — more especially by those who do not play it — it is South Australia."

"The Twinkler", in *South Australian Register*, on arrival of M.C.C. side in Adelaide, November 1924

*

"These are not tests of cricket but tests of the English climate."

Sydney *Guardian*'s comment on three-day Tests in England, prompted by rain-ruined England-Australia Test, Trent Bridge, 1926

*

"There have been a number of tremendous Aboriginal footballers over the years, but only a handful of our cricketers have really made the grade and we've never had a Test player. Producing a Shield and Test player would really bring along the interest."

Vince Copley, co-ordinator of coaching week for Aboriginal boys, Adelaide, January 1987

"There is absolutely nothing at all the matter with cricket as a game. Eliminate the word finance, play it in the spirit of the laws not merely in the letter, and cricket is as delightful as ever."

Major Philip Trevor, 1913

*

"Scotland would stand no chance whatever if pitted against a representative England side, but some interesting games would probably result if a triangular tournament could be arranged between Scotland, Ireland and Wales."

F.S. Ashley-Cooper, 1908

"One thing is quite certain, which is, that the throwing evil is a growing one, and *must* be put down at once, otherwise the very life and spirit of cricket must decay."

"Old Buffer" (F. Gale), 1882

"Our State games have been pushed into the background by almost a continuous succession of Test series since the war and, with the public, at least, they have lost the standing and meaning of other years."

J.H. Fingleton,
on the Sheffield Shield,
1952

*

"The Australian selectors will certainly have to scour the land for fast bowlers to tour England in 1972."

J.A. Snow, 1971.
(Lillee and Massie took 54
Test wickets at 17.72 on the
1972 tour)

*

"Magnificent, magnificent, magnificent. You can't say magnificent too often when you speak of these two batsmen."

Sir Pelham Warner,
on Edrich and Compton,
June 1947

*

"I don't think there could ever have been anyone better than him: he's such a magnificent batsman."

A.W. Greig,
on I.V.A. Richards, 1978

*

"But who, apart from a love of cricket, would make Kennington Oval, surrounded as it is with plain brick houses, with enormous gas-works in full view, the destination of a day's outing?"

The Daily Chronicle on the crowd at the first day of Test cricket in England, 1880

*

"I have been all my life a resolute opponent of any such alteration in the laws of cricket as would affect either the implements used or the law of leg before, but I have at last come round to the view that something has got to be done to help the bowler."

Lord Harris, 1926

*

"By advertising shirts, braces, razor blades, selling his autobiography long before he's ready to write it and organising his benefit fund like a Persian bazaar trader he might just make £5,000 a year.

But this would apply to no more than six out of England's 320 registered county players. More than 200 of them, if they had to rely on their direct income from cricket, would be better off as a bank clerk."

Ian Wooldridge, on the lot of the county cricketer, 1966

"For every Test run I scored, my mother paid me a rupee and my father gave me 100 rupees for every 100 runs I made."

S.M. Gavaskar,
after scoring his 29th Test
century and passing 8,000
Test runs, 1983

*

"At twelve o'clock the clouds were dispersed and King Sol, appearing with all his noonday ardour, sent down propitious rays on the ground, which being rolled, was at two o'clock quite fit for play."

St. Vincent *Sentry*
on St. Vincent XI v Lord
Brackley's XI match, Kings-
town, March 1905

*

"One pronounced advantage from a two-days' match would be this — the gates would almost certainly be larger. You would get more people in two days than you do at present in three days. Matches are too prolonged. We take our pleasures to-day short and sharp; the popularity of football proves this."

Rev. R.S. Holmes,
favouring two-day cham-
pionship cricket, 1911

*

"In 1849, judging from this quaint drawing, the onlookers might be a crowd of shareholders at a company meeting."

Adrian Bury, 1955,
on the water-colour drawing of Kennington Oval by C.J. Basebe of 1849

*

"No claret, no cricket."

Hilaire Belloc,
on being told there was no claret and accordingly departing from a village match in Sussex

*

"I have always believed that there are plenty of good cricketers out there waiting to be found, and that it is up to us to find them."

John Major
(Prime Minister), on the opening at the Oval of the Ken Barrington Centre, 1991

*

"None. I just want to go on playing cricket."

D.K. Lillee,
on being asked his plans for the future, 1979

"I always feel that it was a misfortune when the Cricket Council came to grief. It was a body which could have dealt with abuses effectually. I am convinced that it never would have come to an end if Lord Harris had not gone to India, but it was a difficult thing to carry out properly, and there was no one strong enough to revive it."

John Shuter, 1899

*

"Your Committee feel that the least Unions might be expected to do is to provide proper dressing-room accommodation, bath-rooms, etc., for the convenience of visiting cricketers, whether from overseas or from other centres in this country when Currie Cup Tournaments are being played."

South African Cricket Association annual report for year ended August 31, 1910, on primitive ground arrangements in South Africa

*

"There is too much selfishness on the field to-day, compared with the past, when figures, batting and bowling, were never allowed to interfere with the play of the sportsman, or the advancement of a side as a whole."

A.C. MacLaren, 1922

"They want to show English gentlemen playing their sport in a gentlemanly way."

M.G. de Mellow
(Hambledon C.C.) on a television crew from West Germany attending the village championship final at Lord's (Hambledon v Toft), 1989

*

"We consider that a satisfactory standard was attained in 1939, and we do not believe that any radical changes in the conduct of the game are called for."

Report of M.C.C.
Select Committee, 1944

*

"Scarcely a village now is without its club and its patron, the rich and influential do not shrink from a participation in the pastime with their poorer but not less moral neighbours, and hence Cricketing, as a sport, has been, and is, the greatest and most effective teacher of any on record, from the building of the tower of Babel, down to the demolition of the Crystal Palace."

The Era, rhapsodising on the new cricket season, 1852

*

". . . it was your approach to the game which took root in my mind and which has governed my attitude ever since."

D.C.S. Compton,
in open letter to R.W.V. Robins, 1962

*

"Test cricket has developed into a very solemn business. Very few cricketers really enjoy Test cricket nowadays."

Neville Cardus, 1953

*

"In this age when good manners and courtesy are often disregarded, there *are* more cases of cricketers being given out to the accompaniment of a display of petulance or of bowlers scowling and bad mouthing when their bowling is carted, catches dropped or appeals turned down. We do not want a long queue outside the disciplinary meeting room."

T.A. Sharman,
Hon. Secretary, Lancashire Cricket League, in his annual report on 1990 season, 1991

"Two things he has got right: for a captain who takes his advice, there is a cemetery next to the ground at Taunton, and there will be plenty of volunteers to go on first with the spades. Moreover, there would be no shortage of mourners from our opponents."

R.J.O. Meyer,
in 1948, on a critic's view of
Somerset in 1947 under his
captaincy

*

"It is perfectly safe to state that there are many fine cricketers regularly taking part in these games whose services would be of great value to county and representative cricket were they able to afford the time."

"Second Slip"
(Frank Mitchell), on club
cricket, 1929

*

"Even h'umpires ain't h'invincible."

Unknown umpire's
observation

*

"I don't believe in backing up with one's legs, but I will have to learn to do it. Nearly all the great batsmen often save their wickets in that way."

V.T. Trumper, 1899

*

"In this competition the stronger counties usually take it for granted that they are going to beat the weaker ones, and, regarding the whole affair as a business one, play in a lifeless manner which is a mere travesty of what cricket should be."

George Lacy, on the County
Championship, 1897

*

"A first-rate top-sawyer batsman in form does not require luck to help him against the bowler, but he does need an absence of bad luck — a very different matter, if you think of it."

C.B. Fry, 1903

*

"Club cricket, besides being the most agreeable form of cricket there is both to watch and to play, is a fascinating microcosm of southern English urban middle-class life, with all its jealousies and rivalries and snobbery and the peculiarities of its relations between the sexes."

David Sylvester,
in radio broadcast, 1960

*

"Jack Hobbs was the greatest batsman I ever saw on all wickets, and Victor Trumper the most sheerly brilliant stroke-maker. I would rank both of these ahead of Don Bradman."

F.E. Woolley, 1963

*

"The pitch itself was so studded with small pieces of coral that the ball had to be changed twice in an innings, which lasted about two hours. The mangled balls were brought back as a memento."

E.C. Beete,
of the Demerara (British
Guiana) team, in 1904, on
the pitch in the first inter-
colonial match in the West
Indies (Barbados v De-
merara, Garrison Savannah,
Bridgetown, February 15,
16, 1865)

*

"What can I say? Can't you see how pleased I am?"

A.P.F. Chapman,
captain of England, after
England's victory v Australia
to regain the Ashes,
Oval, 1926

*

"Every run counts the same whether it comes from the cut of a Spooner or the agitated snick through the slips of a No. 8 . . ."

H.V. Hesketh Prichard,
1912

*

"In view of the outstanding performances of their cricket team in the second and third Test Matches, is there any longer any valid reason why the West Indies should not be granted Dominion status?"

Letter in *News Chronicle*,
1950

*

"Apparent lack of enthusiasm is infectious, like cholera, and because of it our cricket shows signs of dying."

Robin Marlar, 1971

*

"The conviction that May cricket is something of a mistake seems to be steadily gaining ground among those who belong to the higher circles of the cricket world."

Baily's Magazine, on the
poor quality of XIs fielded in
May 1879

"It should have happened in Gloucestershire, but Somerset stood in as a willing substitute and host."

R.C. Robertson-Glasgow,
in 1949, on J.B. Hobbs's
1925 equalling and break-
ing at Taunton of W.G.
Grace's number of centuries

*

"I would be perfectly happy to stand in Test matches all year round."

H.D. Bird, 1992

*

"Probably because I play the away-swinger better than most."

E.J. Barlow,
suggesting why he had been
chosen as a "roving ambas-
sador" by South African
cricket and sporting officials, 1984

*

"Like many other examples in this life, umpiring has to be experimented in oneself before one can honestly presume to criticise."

G.A. Faulkner, 1914

*

"The Australians have reduced the practice of making the English three-day match last its full three days to a fine art, and in doing so they have dealt a ruinous blow to the best interests of English cricket."

Westminster Gazette, 1900

*

"Perhaps there is a case for ending the system whereby the President, usually an eminent cricketer, appoints his successor annually, for strengthening the Secretariat, and for making far more use of the International Cricket Conference as an effective policy-making body."

Rex Alston,
on M.C.C., 1968

*

"For goodness sake, Mr. Thornton, serve McIntyre the same."

James Southerton,
on all four balls in an over
being hit by C.I. Thornton
for four, in Gentlemen v
Players match, Brighton,
1871

*

". . . when professionals fail to bowl a single straight ball for overs on end, there is nobody to blame but the men concerned."

E.R. Dexter,
on England's bowlers in
one-day International v
Australia, Lord's, 1972

*

"If a bowler, a man who can bowl at all, is bowling on a bad wicket, it does not matter how a batsman plays, with his leg, with his head, or anything else, he should get him out."

Arthur Shrewsbury, 1893

*

". . . we must all realize there is no disgrace in losing — only in playing bad cricket."

N.J. Contractor, 1961,
on eve of 1961–62 India v
England Test series

"Nothing but fine weather, and, perhaps, we may add, freedom from public anxiety, is necessary to make 1878 an 'epoch-making' season in the history of cricket."

Daily News,
anticipating the 1878 season and the presence of D.W. Gregory's first Australian team

*

"Little praise is given to the bowler these days, but I maintain that Grimmett is a bigger acquisition to Australia than Bradman."

Alan Fairfax, 1932

*

"The Press now give such admirable reports of matches all over the country that thousands do not take the trouble to go even a couple of miles to watch a game."

Lord Hawke, 1914

*

"Pakistan cricket is, of course, an official game. No one should be surprised if they found a cricket net in the gangway of a Pakistan airliner: the airline is famous for cricketers."

Robin Marlar, 1971

"There should be a particular decorum in first–class cricket, and national domestic competitions must be contested with the upholding of cricket's best ideals in mind."

> Gul Hameed Bhatti,
> on irregularities in domestic
> first-class cricket in Pakis-
> tan, 1985

*

"While one man plays county cricket a thousand play Club Cricket, yet we find that all legislation is directed to the regulation of county and instructional cricket. It is county cricket *toujours*. It is county cricket *ad nauseam*."

> *The Cricketer and Football
> Player*, 1906

*

"After seeing the West Indian cricketers in the field at Lord's it is not surprising that they are not winning their matches as we expected them to do, for they apparently have to get the other side out twice in an innings through missing catches."

> "Second Slip"
> (Frank Mitchell), 1928

*

"Virtually all bowlers would have to say that they have tampered with the ball at some stage during their county career."

Angus Fraser,
September 1992

*

"When the English team took the field it might have been a dyer's holiday."

William Mabane, M.P.,
in 1932, on the multi-coloured caps worn in Australia in 1928–29 by the side under A.P.F. Chapman

*

"There is nothing in the world so self-satisfied as the first-class cricketer so long as he is in his prime."

Sir Home Gordon, 1909

*

"Its ill-concealed ridge and furrow appearance reminded one of a reclaimed hop-ground, rather than a billiard-lawn."

"Hillyer",
in 1889, writing of Lord's in 1850

*

"Certainly the improvement in the pitches and in the grounds themselves have been most marked; anyone who has been playing as long as I have could not fail to notice that."

Lord Hawke, 1910

*

"I have done so since I was three!"

B.S. Chandrasekhar,
aged 18, on his throwing
with his left arm and bowling with his right, 1964

*

"I believe the geologists call it decomposed diorite."

George Allsop,
secretary, Wanderers Club,
Johannesburg, on being
asked about the club's soil,
1904

*

"He was, and will remain, the very impersonation of cricket, redolent of fresh air, of good humour, of conflict without malice, of chivalrous strife, of keenness for victory by fair means, and utter detestation of all that was foul."

Sir Arthur Conan Doyle,
of W.G. Grace, 1915

*

"The English cricket essayists have largely blended topography, personal and regional characteristics and impressionism into romantic portraits of the players, portraits which will appeal to the general reader, and possibly to posterity, for their literary qualities rather than as the basis of cricket history. The Australian writers, of whom M.A. Noble and Mr Arthur Mailey have been outstanding, have tended to be well-informed and accurate but not much affected by literary style."

The Times Literary Supplement, 1946

*

"Cricket seems as much a natural aptitude to an Australian as violin playing to a Hungarian."

Neville Cardus, 1947

*

". . . if Trumper cannot come to England, the Australians might as well stop at home."

A.C. MacLaren, 1904, on the possibility of V.T. Trumper not touring England in 1905 through illness

*

"As you visit the great cities of this vast kingdom, independently of the incidents of travel, the recognition of old friends and old-foe acquaintances will not be among the least of the happy circumstances attached to the movements of our little army."

N. Felix,
qua President, in address to
the Eleven of England, 1852

*

"Whether a cricket championship of Europe will ever become *fait accompli* a later generation will know. It would at any rate be a kindlier fight to a finish than that which is warming up as I write."

E.H.D. Sewell,
writing in September 1914

*

"A chasm rather than a gulf separates the club player from the professional."

Ian Wooldridge, 1966

"A Cambridge friend said to me the other day that you saw the same old names year after year playing for their counties, like a lot of old selling platers who appear race after race at the various meetings."

A.C. MacLaren, 1923

*

"The Lancashire League! It was a title which caught my imagination as a fanatical cricketing youngster, and apparently it still has the same fascination for many."

P.I. Philpott,
former Ramsbottom and
East Lancashire profession-
al, 1973

*

"The County Cricket Council, in my opinion, is almost sure to come to life again, and despite all the mud that has been thrown at it, will do useful work."

W.G. Grace, 1891

*

"In Sussex, no difference."

A.E.R. Gilligan,
captain, Sussex C.C.C., on
being asked the difference
between an amateur and a
professional, 1924

"They haven't asked me — and if I suddenly can't get any runs they won't."

K.S. Duleepsinhji,
a few hours before his name
was announced to tour Australia with the M.C.C. side
of 1932—33. (He subsequently did not tour through
ill health)

"Let me reiterate that it is easier to become proficient in fielding than in either bowling or batting."

G.L. Jessop, 1901

*

"When you have a bat or the ball in your hand, it's up to you. There is no point in expecting anybody else to do your job."

A.R. Border,
captain, Australia, November 1985

"If a girl is good enough for the team then there will be a place for her. At this school everything is based on merit."

Dr Ian Walker,
headmaster, King's School,
Rochester, on allowing girls
into the school cricket XI,
1992

*

"He was like a schoolboy with castor-oil. He just took it."

R.C. Robertson-Glasgow,
on D.G. Bradman on a
"sticky" pitch, 1949

*

"The Malayan Cricket Association have arranged for a medicine man to help ensure that rain does not interfere with play during the tour by Worcestershire."

Reuter report, from Kuala
Lumpur, March 1965

*

". . . I'd like to see the best of English umpires officiating in a match with crowds of over 40,000 and come out of it without making mistakes."

S.M. Gavaskar, 1977

"Aubrey Faulkner, the great South African all-round cricketer, once gave his opinion that the difference between English and Australian cricketers was roughly as follows — the Englishman plays as a rule a little below his best form in a Test match, and the Australian plays as a rule a little above."

Neville Cardus, 1953

*

"I cannot help thinking that a great deal would be done to stop slow play — I am not referring to slow play when a draw has to be worked for, because that is quite another thing — if a 'not out' were to count as a complete innings."

E.J. Diver, 1899

*

"Bouncers turn cricket from a game of skill and intellect into a near-brawl. The greatest bowlers of the century — Maurice Tate, Alec Bedser, Clarrie Grimmett, Bill O'Reilly, Hedley Verity, Sydney Barnes, to name only half a dozen — all bowled at the wicket."

Sir Leonard Hutton, 1960

*

"It was the sort of ball a man might see if he was dreaming or drunk."

C.G. Macartney,
on the ball by S.F. Barnes
that bowled V.T. Trumper
in first Test, Sydney,
December 1907

*

"What's the point in 'O' levels? They don't help you play cricket!"

I.T. Botham,
as a schoolboy

*

"You don't make excuses in cricket; you just go back to the nets over and over again and grind the faults out of your game."

Geoffrey Boycott, 1970

*

". . . I have not the slightest sympathy with the man who makes games or athletics the be-all and end-all of life."

F.S. Ashley-Cooper, 1908

*

"In this parched land some things are more important than cricket."

Don Cameron,
on the welcome given to rain in drought-stricken Zimbabwe during the Zimbabwe v New Zealand Test, Bulawayo, November 1992

*

"I really believe Spofforth has forgotten more about bowling than any bowler of to-day knows."

H.V. Hesketh Prichard, 1912

*

"I should say the Lord's wicket is the funniest piece of turf in creation."

"Rover",
in *The Morning Leader*, following the Australians' dismissal for 18 by the M.C.C., Lord's, 1896

*

". . . it is a funny game, and there are many pitfalls for critics."

Hon. R.H. Lyttelton, 1920

"The best innings I ever saw, bar none! It was simply wonderful. And the man had an injured wrist, too!"

H.P. Chaplin (Sussex),
on E.B. Alletson's 189 out
of 227 in 90 minutes for
Nottinghamshire at Hove,
1911

*

"Years ago, a young batsman walked to the wicket at Cheltenham and struck two boundaries from Lancashire bowlers, then lost his wicket. I had seen, from these two strokes, enough. I wrote a quarter of a column about his potentiality. It was Wally Hammond."

Neville Cardus, 1970

*

"Among cricket writers he would have to growl, however churlishly, 'Give me Neville'."

Christopher Wordsworth,
in 1981, contemplating
W.G. Grace's nomination
(Neville Cardus) of the pick
of cricket writers

". . . I believe the real reason why the Australians have gone on winning matches is because the Australians *work* harder at their cricket: the English *play* at the game."

*

"We may live, but cannot win, on pictures and memories and old score-books."

R.C.	Robertson-Glasgow,
1946

*

"Difficult! What fast bowler can be difficult?"

W.G. Grace,
as a young man, on being
asked if a certain player was
"a difficult bowler"

*

"To tell you the truth, when I come to think about bygone times, the reminiscences, as you call 'em, get so mixed and muddled up in my old brains that I can't clearly call 'em to mind at all."

Tom Hearne,
manager of Lord's ground
bowlers, when asked for his
memories, aged 68, 1895

"Australian sides have traditionally drawn their inspiration from the deeds of fellow players and that is why we have become known throughout the cricket world as a team of aggressive competitors. I would hate to see that change."

I.M. Chappell, 1984

*

"I don't think Glenn Turner has any right to come here and criticise our wickets, especially when you see the muck they play on over there."

R.W. Marsh,
responding to criticism of
the WACA pitch by G.M.
Turner, cricket manager of
New Zealand side in Australia, November 1985

*

". . . the image of a Thorpe drawing from a *Punch* summer number."

Denzil Batchelor,
on W.A. Hadlee, 1949

*

"Could I live my youth and early manhood over again, I could wish for nothing better than to play a part in the further development of the national summer game."

Lord Hawke,
aged 53, 1914

". . . as one who has had to face throwing in Australia on fast wickets (faster than any we have in England), I, for one, consider it quite time the matter be taken up before someone else is killed at the wicket."

A.C. MacLaren,
on the "throwing" question,
1900

*

"Shrewd spin bowling, countered by attacking batting, is a more likely antidote for dull play than constant tampering with the laws of the game."

D.C.S. Compton, 1971

*

"We tried to get him out every ball."

M.W. Tate,
on being asked why he and
his fellow bowlers did not
keep D.G. Bradman "quiet"
when he scored 309* in a
day at Headingley in 1930

". . . I have a theory that to be publicly proclaimed as such in Australia is about as fortuitous as being handed the black spot, being branded with the mark of Cain or having the professional kiss of death planted square on your forehead."

Ian Wooldridge,
on Australian players being heralded as "the next Bradman", 1972

*

"But the real question is whether we have made enough runs."

C.B. Fry,
with England's score at 634–5 (of an eventual 903–7 dec.) after two days of the Test v Australia, Oval, 1938

*

"I don't think it is fair to call it a record . . . It is more an achievement. Had Bradman played 95 Tests he would probably have scored 75 centuries."

S.M. Gavaskar,
on equalling (in his 95th Test) D.G. Bradman's record of 29 Test centuries, Delhi, October 1983

*

"There they go, the slowest pair of rungetters in England!"

E.M. Grace,
criticising W.G. Grace taking W.R. Gilbert in with him to score runs against the clock v Surrey at Cheltenham, 1880. (They scored 52-0, to win, in 26 minutes)

*

"It is a pleasant fiction, the belief that the county cricketer whom we see at Lord's, the Oval, Leyton, Bramall-lane, Nottingham, Hove, and the other great cricket grounds of England, are the finest exponents of the game in the country. But it is only a fiction, for there are dozens of men who, were they able to steal the time from their businesses, would to-day be playing for their counties, but who are content to give only their Saturdays and an occasional week-day to the game."

The Cricketer and Football Player, 1906

*

"There is much in modern journalism which a cricketer deplores — particularly the quest of the sensational and the dirty linen of private disputes."

G.D. Martineau, 1936

"Yes, confound the fellow; he doesn't throw now so well as he used to bowl."

A.N. Hornby's
response to an observation
by Capt. Holden (Notting-
hamshire) that A. Watson,
of Lancashire, "throws
now", c.1880

*

"I have got no doubts in my mind that I will be a success in Test cricket and if I didn't believe that I'd be going backwards."

G.A. Hick, December 1991

*

"Of all the great players I have seen, F.E. Woolley, to my mind, is the most attractive and graceful of them all. As an umpire you have to be very cautious, as he hits very straight. He has hit me twice, but fortunate-ly not seriously."

Frank Chester, 1931

*

"One may take it for granted that never again will a Colonial player be procured in order that he may become a member of an English county team."

Major Philip Trevor, 1908

". . . if any match can produce two such cover points as Mr Hedges and Mr Gilbert Ashton, may I be there to see it."

Hon. R.H. Lyttelton,
on the University Match,
1921

*

"What sort of cricket is it that calls for bowlers who don't concede runs and taking wickets is not the primary consideration?"

W.E. Bowes,
on limited-overs cricket,
1969

*

"Mr W.G. Grace is the father of Cricket and the brother of Dr E.M. Grace."

Schoolboy,
at the time of W.G. Grace's
rise to eminence

*

"During lunch I decided it was worth while having a go . . . and the day was ours."

D.G. Bradman,
on the final day of the Test
at Headingley, when Au-
stralia scored 404−3 to
win, 1948

*

". . . it was he, above all others, who taught us the commercial value of the finished match and the exciting third day."

R.C. Robertson-Glasgow,
on B.H. Lyon, 1946

*

"I make so bold as to say that Cowdrey's first innings definitely and once and for all announced that he is the best and most self-possessed young amateur batsman in English cricket since, say, C.F. Walters — though he is not at all like Walters in style."

Neville Cardus,
following M.C. Cowdrey's
110 and 103 for M.C.C. v
New South Wales, Sydney,
November 1954

*

"The championship is my concern. My duty is not to build a side for the future but to win, now."

D.B. Close,
captain, Yorkshire, replying
to captaincy criticism,
1963. (Yorkshire won the
championship)

*

"When they were calling us the Ugly Australians I didn't mind being included, as that title was only gained because we were winning regularly."

R.W. Marsh, 1982

*

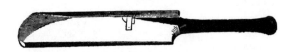

" 'Lobs' are perhaps not always so successful as they might be made, merely because the performer does not practise them sufficiently."

J.N. Crawford, 1908

*

". . . what an opportunity was lost of ascertaining how eminent batsmen would have shaped at lobs during that amicable epilogue at Lord's."

Sir Home Gordon,
on the time-limit game played when the England v
South Africa Test at Lord's
ended early on the third
day, 1951

"Fred Burbidge, who was captain of Surrey in its palmy days, told me that our present eleven would knock that of '65 into a cocked hat. The eleven of last year was, in his opinion, better than the famous one in the days of Julius Caesar, Griffith, Jupp, Caffyn, Mortlock, etc."

C.W. Alcock,
secretary, Surrey, 1893

*

"Each Australian learns something in England, and when he returns the rising generation reaps the benefit of it."

J. Worrall, 1899

*

"I prefer batting on English wickets, the best of which, I think, is at Lord's. Anyhow, it most resembles the Sydney Cricket Ground, and I suppose that is why our fellows usually do pretty well there."

V.T. Trumper, 1905

*

"What a pity he cannot go out to Australia as Fry's liaison officer. As an education agent to the Commonwealth in instructing them how to play cricket, he would be wonderful."

Sir Home Gordon,
on G.J.V. Weigall, 1936

*

"Well, I have been twenty years and more learning."

W.A. Humphreys,
on being asked how long it
would take to learn how to
bowl lobs, 1893

*

"Mr Jessop puts so much force into his mis-hits that the low ones are on to the fielder before he is ready for them, and the ball when it goes high spins so much that it almost loses shape temporarily."

The Morning Post, 1908

*

"I tend to look at sport as a contest between brain and brain rather than technique and technique."

I.M. Chappell, 1982

"It is totally uneven, and that is my main concern. It is difficult to score runs on a wicket full of ridges. Poor wickets mean poor cricket, and everyone wants attractive cricket."

Richie Robinson, captain of Victoria, criticising the Melbourne Cricket Ground wicket, 1980

*

"The quality of the bowlers I have faced from time to time during my career in first-class cricket must, to some extent, be a matter of opinion, but I *know* the bowlers whom I found most difficult to play, and the one I place at the top of the list will no doubt surprise some people. He is Mr J.W.H.T. Douglas, the Essex captain."

J.B. Hobbs, 1925

*

"Only fancy what you would have said five or six years ago if any idiot had suggested to you that in June, 1903, Gloucestershire would lose a match by seven wickets because one W.G. Grace took six of their wickets in the first innings, and then hit up 150 runs against them."

Baily's Magazine, on W.G. Grace's performance for London County v Gloucestershire, Crystal Palace, 1903

*

"Cricketers are made, not born."

W.G. Grace, 1899

*

"I do not think I have ever encountered a more technically perfect batsman than Barry Richards."

T.E. Bailey, 1978

*

"He moved from 0 to 92 as though he were lacerating some jovial Lord's Taverners attack."

Ian Wooldridge,
on K.D. Walters's first Test
innings (155 v England,
Brisbane, 1965–66)

*

"Perhaps we have become so used to the limited overs game that we have simply forgotten the skills of first-class cricket."

K.C. Wessels,
captain, South Africa,
November 1992 (before first
Test v India)

*

"There's a possibility that we will be judged by future generations on our one-day statistics. That is the day I dread most."

A.R. Border,
captain, Australia, December 1992

*

"He had the broadest bat I ever saw and it seemed to be all middle . . ."

Sir Stanley Jackson,
on W.G. Grace

*

"Generally speaking, bowlers do not think enough . . ."

F.R. Spofforth, 1905

*

"Australia and England have put their houses in order. It was time other countries, too, showed a similar respect for the laws and ethics of cricket."

K.N. Prabhu,
on suspect bowling actions,
1968

*

"The enthusiast can spend his winter evenings over cricket books as easily as his summer days in the field."

E.B.V. Christian, 1899

*

"Grace, like Bach, summed up in himself the essential principles, the grammar and fundamental vocabulary of his art."

Neville Cardus, on W.G. Grace, 1948

*

"This type of patient stubbornness is more necessary at a Mons or a Cambrai than a cricket field."

E.H.D. Sewell, on W.H. Denton scoring a century in over seven hours for Northamptonshire v Derbyshire, 1914

*

"We are afraid that even now there are many country parsons who would rather see their parishioners loafing aimlessly or mischievously about the lanes of a Sunday afternoon than engaged in a game of cricket, or skittles, or bowls."

The Academy, 1908

"Name or no name, out you go, and no mercy, when your form shows a sign of autumn."

C.B. Fry,
on Australian cricketers,
1936

*

"We are forced, just now, to have to quote Australia when we want to describe efficiency."

Hon. R.H. Lyttelton, 1921

*

"Don Bradman, who is still ranked as an amateur, has got more out of cricket in the past four years than anyone I know."

Alan Fairfax, 1932

*

"Proficient Test cricketers are not born, they are manufactured by a combination of two things — rigid application and unlimited competitive experience."

Ray Illingworth, 1972

"Any American in London or elsewhere in England yesterday and to-day instantly realised that something had turned the country topsyturvy. Barbers, 'bus conductors, financiers, shopkeepers, policemen, stenographers tripping to and from work, dignified lawyers and vociferous street venders – all had a topic in common which made them kin for the moment."

New York Times,
on J.B. Hobbs surpassing
W.G. Grace's record num-
ber of centuries, 1925

*

"Let me say right away that I have little sympathy with the batsmen of to-day, be they Australians or Englishmen, who cannot stand up to fast bowling. What have they got bats for?"

T.W. Hayward, 1935

*

"All cricket-lovers, whatever their views, may be grateful for the fact that matting wickets give to the game some of its most interesting and colourful personalities."

I.A.R. Peebles,
on South African cricket,
1947

*

"Unless the county clubs do more earnestly nurse amateurism, it is not so very difficult to estimate the days when the Championship will be delivered up to professionalism."

The Observer, 1908

*

"Statistics can be both revealing and misleading."

Sir Donald Bradman, 1992

*

"What England will be like a hundred years hence we cannot pretend to prophesy, but this we can say — that Lord's and the M.C.C. will continue to flourish and increase their popularity."

Lord Hawke
(President, M.C.C.), at
Lord's Centenary Dinner,
1914

"But you can take it from me, we shall never import players from outside the county — unless the time comes when the members throw out the present committee and elect one which will bring in Australians, Indians, Pakistanis, West Indians, New Zealanders, and what have you. I'm sure we can pick a team from within the county that will give the public what they want."

John Temple,
chairman, Yorkshire C.C.C.
cricket   sub-committee,
1972

*

"The best batting on the 'worst' pitch — that's the measure of greatness."

R.C.   Robertson–Glasgow,
1949

*

"Nothing tends to breed irritation quicker among spectators than to see the bad ball played with just as much caution as the really good one."

G.L. Jessop, 1911

*

"Only on dull days and in dull places is cricket dull."

Neville Cardus, 1923

*

"If you don't score runs you don't expect to play and that's all there is to it."

A.J. Lamb,
on not being selected by
England for the final Test v
West Indies, 1991

*

"Wonderful as I believe the champion to have been, I do not for a moment think that we have yet reached the maximum in batting . . ."

Major Philip Trevor,
on W.G. Grace, 1913

*

"Anything I say would only create another uproar."

Harold Larwood,
on being asked if he would
play for England v Australia
in the second Test of 1934 if
fit and invited, at Horsham,
June 12, 1934

*

"I enjoy fast bowling, although you have second thoughts when you are not taking wickets."

D.K. Lillee, 1972

*

"Six 150s for Hampshire by the end of May should do it."

D.I. Gower,
in Bombay, February 1993,
on his prospects of regain-
ing his Test place in 1993

*

"It's victory for persecutor Gubby Allen."

Rand Daily Mail
(Johannesburg)   headline,
June 29, 1960, after G.M.
Griffin had been withdrawn
as a bowler on the South
African tour of England

"Cricket develops the mind; there is more *thinking* to be done over cricket than over any other game."

A.C. MacLaren, 1905

*

"Why should not the stumps at cricket, like the targets at archery, be closer together or wider apart, according to the proficiency of the players?"

Rev. James Pycroft, 1876

*

"It has all the dignity of a streetfight and about as much cerebral strategy as noughts and crosses."

Ian Wooldridge,
on the six-a-side international cricket tournament in Hong Kong, 1993

*

"Mr Beloe and gentlemen, I sincerely thank you. I hope you will excuse me from saying more, as I have a long afternoon before me."

W.G. Grace's
speech of thanks, 1895, on being congratulated by Mr Harry Beloe (President, Gloucestershire C.C.C.) during the luncheon interval v Somerset, Bristol, on completing his 100th first-class century, during his 288

"I honestly think they can be beaten."

A.W. Greig
(captain of England) of the
West Indies, prior to the
Test series of 1976 (West
Indies won 3−0, with two
draws)

*

"It is futile to ignore the luck element in cricket. In fact, no cricketer ever does ignore it."

E.H.D. Sewell, 1908

*

"I wouldn't swap the MCG mob for two Viv Richards or three Michael Holdings."

D.K. Lillee,
on his affection for the Melbourne crowd, 1982

*

"Take a Chance. Come in for an Hour. Have a Cup of Tea or a Glass of Beer, or Both. Never Mind the Rain. Play May Start at Any Time. All Day Licence."

Suggested notice for outer
walls of cricket grounds,
R.C. Robertson-Glasgow,
1946

"I'm lost for words."

*

"Duleep told me that whenever he had to call on the Prime Minister to discuss matters of international affairs, it was always half an hour before any business was discussed, as cricket was the sole topic."

*

"I consider myself to be a very simple person. I'd be just as happy to keep away from bloody trouble and controversy, but I've got my opinions and once I'm asked for them I give them."

"England do not so much attract crowds these days as mourners at a funeral . . ."

Martin Johnson,
cricket correspondent of *The Independent*, with England 2−0 down in the series v Australia, 1993

*

"It was like seeing Rubinstein playing to two cleaners and 10,000 empty seats."

Ian Wooldridge,
on G.S. Sobers batting for Nottinghamshire v Middlesex before a very small crowd at Lord's, 1972

*

"I wish I had had certain modern batsmen to bowl at before I gave up."

George Freeman, 1894

*

"The fact that revisions are needed at this stage, nearly 160 years after the first issue of M.C.C. laws in 1788, shows that the game is still growing and capable of further development, which from a Marxist point of view, is noteworthy."

Daily Worker, 1947

"In my opinion cricket is too great a game to think about statistically . . ."

E.H. Hendren, 1928

*

"No, mummy, but it will make my cricket bat wet."

M.A. Atherton, aged six, on a seaside holiday, in reply to a parental assurance that the water would not harm him

*

"I'd rather not say anything. I don't want to be quoted. I want to keep my opinions to myself."

J.M. Brearley, on being asked how he would perform E.R. Dexter's job, June 1993

*

"To me, cricket and England are eternally inseparable."

Roy Hattersley, 1983

*

"Clive Rice and Notts go together like fish and chips."

C.H. Lloyd, 1985

*

"The idea of defeat never occurred to us. We hoped in a kindly, charitable way that the Australians would make a creditable show, as otherwise we feared their tour would be a failure."

Sydney Pardon
in 1914 on the M.C.C. v
Australians match at Lord's,
1878, won by the Austra-
lians in a single day by nine
wickets

*

"A cricketer's age is not numbered by years but by seasons."

G.L. Jessop, 1926

*

"You're not starting all that nonsense again at your age, are you?"

Mrs T.W. Graveney,
on hearing the news of her
husband's recall to Test
cricket at the age of 39 after
an interval of over three
years, 1966

"To see this man Sobers so gracefully and easily punching 4's to all corners of the ground, be it against spin or pacemen, made even an old cricket salt like myself sit back and stare in blank disbelief and wonder."

K.R. Miller,
on G.S. Sobers' 113 for
West Indies v Australia at
Sydney, February 1969

*

"With the young players we have coming on in Yorkshire it will be another 50 years before you win again."

Lord Hawke,
congratulating Lord Harris
on Kent winning the County
Championship, 1913. (Kent
next won 57 years later, in
1970)

*

". . . Christ's disciples were just ordinary men. In Australia the test match is being played now and England's captain is Wally Hammond. A captain leads a team and his men follow him — *what Wally Hammond is to England today Christ was to the early Christians.*"

BBC Light Programme,
Sunday, February 9, 1947

"I believe you can't be good at anything unless you know the history of the game. One of the things I find extraordinary is the modern player hardly reads anything about the history of the game."

A.V. Bedser, 1985

*

"I want to be the Geoff Boycott of Surrey, and as valuable to my side."

Younis Ahmed, 1972

*

"It will be a bad day for English cricket when the amateur finally retires from first-class engagements, but signs are not wanting that this will be the case unless trouble is taken in some degree to meet his convenience."

Saturday Review, 1900

*

"They played shots as if they were at a gunfight in the old days of the Wild West."

S.M. Gavaskar,
on India's batsmen, after In-
dia's defeat in third Test v
South Africa, Port Elizabeth,
December 1992

"The one thing that strikes me about the average crowd — and this is more true of the South than the North — is its ignorance, its startling and fathomless ignorance, of the game in general, and the match that is going on in particular."

Dudley Carew, 1928

*

"I have no qualification whatever to write about Kent cricket, but as no qualification is nowadays the best qualification when the subject is cricket, I shall struggle in a goodly company."

E.H.D. Sewell,
writing on Kent Cricket,
1908

*

"Mike Denness has as much claim to Illingworth's job as the vice-captain of Stoke Poges's second eleven."

Michael Parkinson, 1972

"Some of these lads must have passports thicker than the London A–Z."

Martin Johnson,
on the year-round commit-
ments of some West Indian
cricketers, 1994

*

"I think that any bowler who pitches a ball less than half-way ought to be no-balled without appeal, because he becomes dangerous to the batsman, who goes in with a fear of being seriously hurt."

J.B. Wostinholm,
secretary, Yorkshire C.C.C.,
1895

*

"Either because players are more restrained or because the Wisbech and District, Cambridgeshire, Cricket League is more broadminded, the League's rule against obscene language on the field has been deleted."

Daily Mirror, 1946

*

"Cricket is really in a sad state. The main problem is that they take it all so seriously. They don't seem to be enjoying it."

R.E.S. Wyatt,
aged 91, February 1993

" 'Have you seen the champion?' That was the question I often heard asked in my early boyhood. Men did not say 'the cricket champion' – but just 'the champion'. There was only one."

Major Philip Trevor,
on W.G. Grace, 1913

*

". . . if you can time the ball correctly you can play almost anyhow, and make your centuries."

C.B. Fry, 1905

*

"I don't know that Test cricket can be saved. I hope so, but I'm not convinced."

Lynton Taylor,
managing director, PBL Marketing, 1982

*

"Is this much-vaunted English type of instant cricket good for the country's Test soul? We shall soon see . . ."

J.H. Fingleton,
May 1972 (the Test series that summer was shared)

*

"County cricket became so slow that people stopped watching it. Now Test cricket has become slower and slower and people are staying away from that too."

Leslie Deakins,
secretary, Warwickshire
C.C.C., 1960

*

"Although a Tory of the most pestilent description, I would rather see a village possess a cricket club than a Conservative association; if there be a village without one there is something rotten in the state of that place."

Gerald Fiennes, 1893

*

"Botham? . . . I could have bowled him out with a cabbage, with the outside leaves on."

C.G. Pepper
(New South Wales)

*

"The only fault I have to find with umpires in England (if fault it can be termed) is that they are far too hard on bowlers."

G.A. Faulkner, 1914

"If I could get 236 Test wickets with in-swing, what might he have achieved with a much more dangerous ball cutting away? He was always as good as I was."

A.V. Bedser,
in 1972, on his brother E.A., who gave up, in his teens, bowling out-swingers

*

"If it was our flamin' lot, they'd be thrown off the Sydney Harbour Bridge."

J.R. Thomson,
on England's cricket hierarchy, after England's innings defeat v Australia at Lord's, 1993

*

"No space now for batting and bowling averages. Cricket (and playing the game) was an English tradition — too clean and wholesome, I fear, for the Socialist dictators."

Letter in *Sunday Express*, 1947

*

"Now, you cannot make omelettes without breaking eggs, and you cannot have fast bowling without occasional knocks."

W.A. Bettesworth, 1927

"I was always a yard faster when the guy at the other end was wearing the three lions and the crown on his sweater!"

D.K. Lillee, 1993

*

"The 'Neue Freie Presse' (Vienna) to-day says it is not believed that the Ottoman Government will persist in its demand for the restoration of the old Oval — Surrey, 70 for 4."

Typographical commixture
in the Globe, May 20, 1897

*

"By a printer's error I was made last week to refer to Richardson's 'pale face'. It should have been 'great pace'!"

Cecil Headlam, 1922

*

"I'd rather have a bowler who can bowl a length than one who can run around the ground 10 times."

Raymond Illingworth,
on the day he was
appointed chairman of the
England selectors, 1994

*

"Thank goodness, there are still left to us a few, a very few, journals whose cricket correspondents do not invariably consider success in a Test Match as a superhuman achievement, and failure as outrageous and culpable incompetence."

R.C. Robertson-Glasgow,
1930

*

"However good the individual is, you only get there by hard work. You don't just *become* great."

K.W.R. Fletcher, 1993

"In the next twelve months we shall be building up an eleven to meet Australia in Australia, and it is certain that we shall have no success against our formidable adversaries unless our team is imbued with the highest possible enthusiasm and discipline. Nothing less will suffice."

P.F. Warner,
on the forthcoming
1932–33 M.C.C. tour of
Australia, May 1931

"Good mornin' gen'tlemen."

Traditional greeting by Wesley Hall on turning to the press box after marking out his run-up and finishing a few yards from the boundary

*

"It would be a serious blow to English cricket if every promising young bowler sacrificed spin to swerve; as an assistance to a length bowler the latter is of the greatest value, but as a match winning factor it can never rank with the former."

H.S. Altham, 1913

*

"I felt a lot safer in the press box, for the bowling looked very dangerous stuff."

J.B. Hobbs,
on the dismissal of Bradman
(b Larwood 13), Australian
XI v M.C.C., Melbourne,
November 1932

*

"I felt like an executioner pressing the button."

Umpire Karl Liebenberg,
after giving S.R. Tendulkar
out via a television replay,
Durban, 1992

"My fingers feel like I've been playing the piano for 10 hours straight. We all feel like we've been banged around inside a coconut shell."

D.M. Jones (Australia),
following the third Test v
West Indies at Melbourne,
December 1988

*

". . . there are normally at least three in every team."

T.E. Bailey,
on batsmen who never be-
lieve they are out, 1966

*

"Let him learn to be a good skipper first and worry about being an authority on batsmen later."

W.J. O'Reilly,
on I.T. Botham, on Botham
declaring I.V.A. Richards to
be "a better player" than
D.G. Bradman, 1981

*

"Experience is worth a hell of a lot, and more so in cricket than in any other game."

Raymond Illingworth,
chairman of England selectors, 1994

"Inspiriting as is the presence of a crowd, cricket is just as great a game when watched by 500 people as by 20,000. All its fine points would be lost if nothing were considered beyond the desire of the spectators for constant excitement."

Daily Telegraph, 1906

*

"It is not necessary to wait on the score-board to arrive at a proper valuation of a Pollock, a Richards, any more than it is necessary to listen to a Kreisler, a Menuhin, a Beecham, for a whole movement. Class is immediately communicated."

Neville Cardus, 1970

*

"In culinary terms, we are about to start a formal, dinner-jacketed, six-course banquet (the Ashes) with a chimps' tea-party, where the yardstick is not so much haute cuisine as the amount of jelly and ice-cream dripping from the wall-paper."

Martin Johnson,
of *The Independent*, before
the start of the one-day Internationals between Eng-
land and Australia, May
1993

"I never go to the ground without half-expecting to see Billy Barnes come out of the old public-house at the corner, with Flowers and Sharpe."

Neville Cardus,
on Trent Bridge, 1938

*

"Back foot play is lazy. It is the easy way to try to play fast bowling. It is also the fatal way."

Sir Leonard Hutton,
on the South Africans in England, 1960

*

"Sometimes the catches which look the finest are more surprising to the fieldsman than to the spectators, who of course do not know how nearly he has been to missing them."

Frank Sugg, 1896

*

"Cricket is as subject as business to Parkinson's Law and the play expands to fill the time available."

H.A. Pawson, 1972

"It is quite likely that more sixes were struck here in a single day yesterday than had been hit in Roses matches between Yorkshire and Lancashire since World War I."

Ian Wooldridge,
on the six-a-side international cricket tournament in
Hong Kong, 1993

*

"I'm confident they play the game in Heaven. Wouldn't be Heaven otherwise, would it?"

Patrick Moore,
TV astronomer, 1989

*

". . . there is no secret to account for the success of Yorkshire; all we have done is to play cricket in a way which has won us countless tributes of approval."

Lord Hawke, 1904

*

"Cricket is not what it used to be. Television has changed it and, probably, saved it."

Sydney Morning Herald
leader, 1981

*

"When it comes to cricket, I speak my mind."

Geoffrey Boycott, 1994

*

"Cricket has changed dramatically over the past 20 years and it would be foolish not to make use of television to improve the game. There are photo finishes in horse racing, so why not give the same facility to umpires?"

K.R. Miller,
in February 1981, more than a decade before television cameras were adopted to assist umpires

"It might well be that shirts of cranberry, coral and crimson secure cricket's economic future but at the same time they will have done much to destroy its character and spirit."

Michael Herd,
London *Evening Standard* columnist, on coloured clothing in the Sunday league for the approaching season, April 1993

"Ball-tampering, one way or another, has gone on since cricket has been played."

Imran Khan, 1993

*

"I say, Jack, that chap ought never to get bowled out. You see, he allus plays with three bats — the wooden un and them two pads — besides a bit of carcase shoved in occasionally."

Spectator on A. Shrewsbury
and his pad-play during his
106 for England v Australia,
Lord's, 1893

*

"It was the kind of thing that was interesting to read about and talk about but not to see."

Major Philip Trevor
in 1913 on the batting of
Shrewsbury and Gunn at
Trent Bridge

*

"Just as people look to Kent for their hops and apples they have come to assume that we shall put young wicket-keepers on the counter as well. I wish I knew why it is."

M.C. Cowdrey, 1978

"At the time of writing there is hardly one first-class amateur bowler in England; and, in my opinion, laziness is one of the great causes of this . . ."

F.R. Spofforth, 1905

*

"Boys learn from watching the great players in action. That is what I did. I have never read a coaching book in my life."

B.C. Lara, May 1994

*

". . . your career is only so long as selection committees permit."

E.R. Dexter, 1978

*

"It has always been recognised that 'captaincy' can make or mar a side, but probably never in the history of the game has one man's influence been so generously reflected, his tact and temper so readily responded to, as in the case of the present Yorkshire leader."

P.F. Warner,
on Lord Hawke, 1902

*

"A few there are who cannot hear the melody of cricket, who have never yet listened to the full symphony in the perfect setting of the village green, who think, unhappy mortals, all cricket dull. Dull! There is no dullness save in their own minds."

John Armitage, 1933

*

"There are good rewards for being an international cricketer these days but I'd honestly play for my country if we didn't get paid a penny."

A.J. Stewart, 1994

*

"It is cricket's special charm that the way in which individuals play should be an expression of their own personality and character. The more diversity there is the better."

H.A. Pawson, 1971

*

"Cricket used to be run by a club; it is now run by a committee which makes the Treasury seem like a spontaneous and responsive institution."

Lord Rees-Mogg,
on the first-class game in
England, 1993

"A dangerous meal, lunch. I have known men bowl like angels before it, and roll on to the field like gorged pythons afterwards."

N.A. Knox (Surrey), 1907

*

". . . Mailey's success was due more to his ability to make a cricket ball behave rather like a tennis ball than to any orthodox concentration upon length."

P.G.H. Fender, 1930

*

"Positions numbers 1−11, I would say."

G.P. Howarth,
New Zealand cricket manager on tour of England, 1994, when asked where the side's batting problems lay, on May 14

*

"Bring in the grave–diggers. Dig up the pitches and save us from these run gluts."

K.R. Miller,
on Australian pitches that produced an excess of runs at the start of M.C.C.'s 1962−63 tour of Australia, November 1962

"Five or ten years!"

A.P. Freeman,
when asked how long the
cultivation of length took for
a bowler, 1938

*

"I don't know what I'd do without it. I can imagine nothing more boring than standing in the outfield by the 'Hill' all day without a word being said."

A.W. Greig,
on the comment of specta-
tors on the 'Hill' at Sydney,
1976

*

"Just as the elusive charm of cricket is scarcely to be captured in words, so the joy of watching cricket is quite incommunicable."

Sir Norman Birkett, 1952

*

"There can be no doubt that the grounds in Australia, at Sydney, Melbourne, and Adelaide are better arranged for spectators and players than those in England, and that we shall have in the end to follow their example."

George Lohmann, 1896

"The best way to lead a side is with 500 runs behind you."

G.A. Gooch, 1993

*

"The object of batting is to make runs — to put the ball where no one expects it."

E.M. Grace

*

"Club cricket in this country is too magnificently disorganised to ever do itself justice or reach anything above hopeless mediocrity in standard of play."

Dr L.O.S. Poidevin, 1910

*

"Cricket presents tactical complexities undreamt of on the football pitch; it is chess compared to tiddly-winks."

Times leader, 1993

"You can talk about tactics and attacking fields, but there's nothing like the inspiration of a large crowd behind you."

A.W. Greig, 1976

*

". . . I still don't think I am batting as well as I can."

B.C. Lara,
on June 6, 1994, immediately after his innings of 501 not out for Warwickshire v Durham at Edgbaston

*

"Only by winning can our guys experience the good things in life. It keeps them hungry."

I.V.A. Richards,
on West Indian cricketers, 1993

*

"My theory is that from the moment an Australian youth goes into club cricket he at once finds himself amongst the masters. In England a man might easily take part in good-class Saturday afternoon cricket all his life and never once come into contact with a Test Match player."

Neville Cardus, 1947

"I never knew any other captain who ever succeeded in scoring a point off him, and that means a lot to a side."

G.G. Hearne,
on Lord Harris, 1893

*

"If he can get 100 per cent performance out of the other 10, a captain is worth his place."

Ray Illingworth, 1975

*

"Beefy treats rehearsals like net practice – he doesn't bother."

David English,
on I.T. Botham, during a
national film show and talk
tour by Botham and I.V.A.
Richards, 1992

*

"It seems to me that there is just as much danger in standing up against fast bowling as there is in travelling by an express train or riding in a motor-car. It looks very risky, but there are so few accidents that they are scarcely worthy of consideration."

J.J. Kotze, 1907

"You know, speed is only relative, and the more you get behind the ball the less fast it seems to be coming at you."

G.S. Sobers, 1963

*

"To bat well in a Test match you must have sound technique, character and courage. How can a lad develop technique if he has to swish away in one-day cricket?"

Geoffrey Boycott, 1981

*

"Threats to cricket are so commonplace that I suppose everyone must be getting inoculated against them. After all, as the more historically minded may tell one another, the game has been dying since about 1902."

E.W. Swanton, 1966

*

"They go over there and all that happens is they face bowlers who are really 'pie throwers'."

R.W. Marsh,
on young Australian cricketers who play county cricket in England, 1993

"The outstanding blot on English cricket to-day is the lack of hitting, solely because batsmen are getting back on to their wicket to balls pitched well up to them."

A.C. MacLaren, 1923

*

"There is a time-honoured English tradition of lifting the seam. It happens everywhere — in club cricket, on the village green, in county cricket and Test cricket."

David Lloyd, 1994

*

"He used to lie awake at night cogitating and maturing his plans. He had an absolutely marvellous command over the ball."

W.L. Murdoch,
on F.R. Spofforth, 1900

*

"Will they wear an N.R.B. badge, supported by a signed certificate of incompetence?"

Daily Telegraph leader on proposed legislation on "non-recognised batsmen" and bouncers, 1976

*

"We used to play four-day cricket in my day — but it only took us three days."

A.V. Bedser, 1993

*

"Test Matches nowadays command too much attention and have been too blatantly written up in a certain section of the Press."

G.J.V. Weigall, 1935

*

"What will fill up the stands at both Test and county grounds, and have sponsors and television companies queueing up to do business, is a Test series in which England does really well, not just better than expected. In crude marketing terms, the English cricket industry has to have a product which the public wants to buy."

Times leader, 1990

*

"The average-monger does neither help the side nor entertain the spectators. He is a nuisance, and should be banished."

W.R. Cuttell
(Lancashire), on cricketers
who play for themselves

"Cricket casts a spell over its votaries, as a rule, but this is not invariably true of the professional who may be a first-class player or a fine workman and still not be under the charm."

J.A.H. Catton, 1925

*

"Cricket for cricketers; journalism for journalists."

F.C. Toone,
secretary, Yorkshire C.C.C.,
on condemning the writing
by cricketers in the Press,
1911

*

"Ah, but you must remember that I'm 85."

Sir Donald Bradman,
explaining why he thought
he would average only "50
or 60" against the current
England bowling, March
1994

*

"The first century I ever made was for the Clapham Wanderers (now the Wanderers), at Penshurst, in Kent, fourteen years ago. I got 148, and was missed fifteen times."

D.L.A. Jephson, 1900

"I had the 10th operation of my career 10 weeks ago, and I think my body is starting to tell me something."

I.T. Botham,
aged 37, April 1993

*

"After thirty years of cricket I'm still learning."

A.P. Freeman,
in a radio broadcast, 1938
(with 3,776 first-class wickets to his credit)

*

"Some become arrogant, many difficult. Some forever will remain social misfits. It doesn't concern them. Their only concern is staying on board the team because the alternative is anonymity."

Ian Wooldridge,
on West Indian Test cricketers, 1994

*

". . . one can only meditate on the melancholy standard of a once-great first-class competition."

W.J.O'Reilly,
aged 74, on Sheffield Shield cricket, 1980

"A bat that is perfection to W.G. Grace is useless in the hands of W.G. Quaife, and *vice versa.*"

C.B. Fry,
on the importance of select-
ing a proper bat, 1899

*

"In cricket, today is always the most important day."

Angus Fraser, 1993

*

"There are probably more Englishmen of all ages, trades, professions, classes and types who can go on reading innumerable columns about cricket than about any other subject."

Robert Lynd, 1930

INDEX

The names are those of the persons quoted.

Duleepsinhji, K.S., 81

Elizabeth II, H.M. Queen, 7
English, D., 136

Fairfax, A.G., 74, 87, 102
Faulkner, G.A., 5, 7, 35, 71, 119
Felix, N., 79
Fender, P.G.H., 50, 132
Fiennes, G., 119
Fingleton, J.H.W., 60, 118
Fletcher, K.W.R., 122
Ford, W.J., 20, 30
Fraser, A.R.C., 76, 142
Freeman, A.P., 133, 141
Freeman, G., 111
Fry, C.B., 10, 12, 68 90, 102, 118, 142

Gale, F., 31, 59
Gardiner, A.G., 8
Garrett, T.W., 4
Gavaskar, S.M., 62, 82, 90, 115
Getty, J.P. II, 26
Gibson, A., 56
Gilligan, A.E.R., 9, 80, 110
Gimblett, H., 1, 53
Goldman, J.W., 12
Gooch, G.A., 134
Gordon, Sir Home, 34, 47, 57, 76, 95, 97
Gower, D.I., 107
Grace, Dr. E.M., 34, 91, 134
Grace, Dr. W.G., 80, 87, 99, 108
Graveney, Mrs. T.W., 113
Greig, A.W., 60, 109, 133, 135
Griffith, S.C., 31, 38, 55
Gutteridge, L.E.S., 5, 26, 35

Hall, W.W., 123
Harris, Lord (4th Baron), 3, 6, 49, 61
Harvey, R.N., 11
Haslam, M.J., 23
Hatteresley, R.S.G., 112

Hawke, Lord (7th Baron), 2, 4, 33, 45, 51, 74, 77, 88, 104, 114, 127
Hayward, T.W., 8, 56, 103
Headlam, C., 121
Hearne, G.G., 136
Hearne, T., 87
Hendren, E.H., 6, 112
Herd, M., 128
Hesketh Prichard, H.V., 70, 85
Hick, G.A., 35, 92
Hobbs, (Sir) J.B., 2, 8, 29, 98, 123
Holmes, Rev. R.S., 16, 23, 53, 62
Hornby, A.N., 92
Howard, C.G., 42
Howarth, G.P., 132
Howitt, W., 25
Humphreys, W.A., 97
Hutchinson, H.G., 41, 55
Hutton, (Sir) L., 83, 126

Illingworth, R., 102, 121, 124, 136

Jackson, (Sir) F.S., 100
Jardine, D.R. 45
Jephson, D.L.A., 140
Jessop, G.L., 54, 81, 105, 113
Johnson, M., 111, 117, 125
Johnston, B.A., 40
Jones, D.M., 124

Keating, F., 15
Khan, Imran, 31, 45, 129
Kilburn, J.M., 17
Knox, N.A., 132
Kotze, J.J., 136

Lacy, G., 20, 26, 46, 68
Lamb, A.J., 15, 106
Langford, A.W.T., 17
Lara, B.C., 130, 135
Larwood, H., 3, 107
Liebenberg, K.E., 123
Lillee, D.K., 63, 107, 109, 121
Lloyd, C.H., 113
Lloyd, D., 138